The Yorkshire Dales Library — 3

A History of Swaledale

by

Edmund Cooper

Dalesman Books

1973

£1.00

The Dalesman Publishing Company Ltd.,
Clapham (via Lancaster), Yorkshire

First Published 1973
© Edmund Cooper 1973
ISBN: 0 85206 193 5

The front cover photograph of October sunshine on the slopes of Kisdon, upper Swaledale, is by Geoffrey N. Wright. All other photographs except where stated are from the author's collection. Those on the back cover show:- Top: Muker Band leading the judges to the village show ground about 1910. Bottom: Muker Show 1910. The title page vignette is by Jocelyn M. Campbell.

The Yorkshire Dales Library is a series of specialist studies of aspects of the Dales. Volumes already published are:-

1. 'Malham and Malham Moor' by Arthur Raistrick
2. 'Village Schools: An Upper Wharfedale History' by Elizabeth Raistrick

———————

Printed in Great Britain by Galava Printing Co., Ltd.
Hallam Road, Nelson, Lancs.

Contents

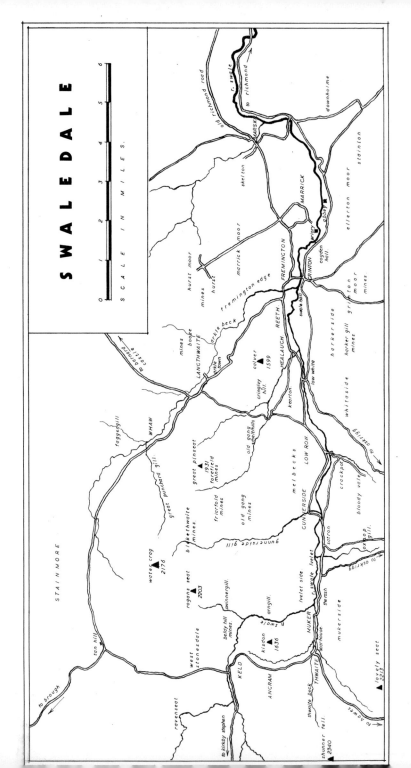

PREFACE

BELIEVING THAT visitors to the Yorkshire Dales National Park, as well as people living there, would welcome a history of Swaledale, I offer them this book. I have tried to give the reader new material which has come my way, in order, as far as possible, not to repeat what has already been written about the dale. I wish to thank many local friends for the help which they have given me, especially those who have lent me photographs, viz: Tom Peacock and Reginald Place of Reeth; Lawrence Barker of Healaugh; Rev. C.B. Bardsley, Cooper Peacock and the late W. Simm Raw of Muker; and David Hall of Burtersett.

The information contained in chapter seventeen on "Reeth in the Nineteenth Century" was mostly taken from a talk given by John Fothergill (1839 - 1911) in about 1902. Chapter sixteen, "The Corpse Way", was originally an article I wrote for "The Dalesman" and is included with permission of its publishers. Acknowledgements are made to the Sheffield University Library for the quotations from Dr. Reaney's "Dictionary of British Surnames"; also to M. Matthews, author of "The Origin of English Surnames" and to Professor R.M. Wilson of Sheffield University.

Edmund Cooper 1973

BOOKS AND MANUSCRIPTS CONSULTED

A. Raistrick   "Pre-History of Yorkshire"

Ekwall   "Oxford Dictionary of English Place Names"

Victoria County History (North Riding)

Bridlington Priory Chartulary

Rievaulx Abbey Chartulary

"Lay Subsidy Rolls for Yorkshire"
                    (Yorks. Archaeological Soc; Record Series Vol. XXI)

P.H. Reaney   "Dictionary of British Surnames"

H. Speight   "Romantic Richmondshire"

Swale Family Papers

Philip Swale Papers (County Record Office, Northallerton)

Kirkby's Inquest

E.R. Wharton   "The Whartons of Wharton Hall"

B. Dale   "The Good Lord Wharton"

North Riding Quarter Sessions Records

E.R. Fawcett   Lead Mining Notes

Raistrick & Jennings   "A History of Lead Mining in the Pennines"

A. Raistrick   "Mines and Miners of Swaledale"

John Harland   "Swaledale Glossary"
                    (Eng. Dialect Society Series C. 1875)

E. Cooper   "Muker, the Story of a Yorkshire Parish"

Muker Parish Papers

Muker Parish Registers

Analysis of Census Returns, 1851
                    (Compiled by the Reeth W.E.A. Local History Class — 1969-70 Tutor: R.T. Fieldhouse)

Harland Papers

York Railway Museum Records

The Wensleydale Advertiser — 1845-49
                    (County Record Office, Northallerton)

Wright   "English Dialect Dictionary"

J. Sutcliffe Smith   "Music of the Yorkshire Dales"

Barker Family Records (J.L. Barker, Healaugh)

Margaret Batty   "Gunnerside Chapel and Gunnerside Folk" (1967)

John Ward   "Methodism in Swaledale" (1865)

HISTORICAL NOVELS

Thomas Armstrong   "Adam Brunskill" — 1952
                    (about the lead miners in the 19th Century)

H.F.M. Prescott   "The Man on a Donkey" 1952
(describes life at Marrick Priory just before
its Dissolution)

The Pre-History of Swaledale

AT THE END of the last glacial period, which had continued for 90,000 years, the polar ice-cap, hundreds of feet in thickness, covered most of Northern Britain. Its maximum encroachment southwards was to a line roughly drawn between the Bristol Channel and the Wash. This limit had fluctuated from time to time as minor recessions took place. In its later phases the land was ice-free as far as Mid-Yorkshire and the East Coast. During the long glacial period so much water was tied up as ice that the oceans of the world were 300 feet below the present level, so that, physically, England was still attached to the Continent of Europe. One could cross over what are now the Straits of Dover on dry land. The southern half of the North Sea was a vast plain of flat marshy land and forest through which the Rhine and Thames flowed northwards.

The country immediately to the south of the Ice-cap was cold and misty. There was little vegetation except for a few stunted willows and birches growing in a moss-covered, tundra-like landscape. Reindeer and other arctic animals browsed upon the moss and scanty herbage which covered the ice-free fringes of the packed ice.

It was in pursuit of these animals that primitive men came to Britain throughout the last ice-age. They had learnt how to fashion tools of stone, wood, antler and bone. Their most useful implement was the flint hand-axe, a core tool. It was shaped by chipping flakes from a round chunk of flint. Flint axes have been found in many parts of Southern Britain, chiefly along the margin of the river Thames and its estuary, where they are particularly abundant. The number of these so-called *Palaeolithic* or *Early Stone Age* men hunting on English soil is supposed not to have exceeded a few hundred at any one time. But they had been coming for thousands of years and as stone implements rarely deteriorate these have accumulated. A few core tools have been found near the Yorkshire coast.

Between approximately 12,000 and 10,000 BC a change of climate occurred. It was the beginning of a warmer period. The vast ice sheets spread over most of the northern hemisphere were receding. Glaciers flowing from the mountain areas had scraped along with them great quantities of boulder clay, gravel and stones. This material was suspended in the ice, and, in addition, the edges of the glaciers were covered with rocks of all sizes which had fallen from the sides of the valleys when frost action and erosion took place. As the temperature rose the glaciers started to melt. Depending upon fluctuations of heat and cold, the snout or nose of a glacier would drop its load of debris at intervals in the form of a bank. These are called terminal moraines. Moraines blocking a valley would eventually create dammed-up lakes.

The melting glacier which flowed down Swaledale left behind morainic deposits which hindered the flow of the melt-waters. So the dale bottom became a series of marshy lakes. These lasted until the river Swale had made for itself a bed deep enough to break through the moraines and drain the water away. One has only to see the dale during winter, when the flooded meadows remind one of what it might have looked like in the past. The most important lakes occurred just above the moraines deposited below Grinton bridge, Howe Hill (above Low Whita bridge), Ivelet, Usha Gap and Keld. The Keld moraine proved to be too formidable and the Swale which formerly flowed to the west of Kisdon, via Angram and Thwaite, made a new channel through the limestone strata between Kisdon and Beldy Hill, thus providing us with the beauty of Catrake and Kisdon falls and its chaotic grandeur of rock and cliff.

Before bridges were built for pack-horses and wheeled traffic, the moraines made suitable fording places. The lakes in the bottom teemed with fish and water fowl. Eventually they silted up and became large swamps through which meandered the river Swale. On each side grew tangled forest trees, alders and ash, providing cover for bears and wolves. Above, upon the steep fell slopes and moors, the forest turned into a scrub of birch and hazel, followed by red pine, mountain ash and thorn. Amongst these were areas of rough grass, the feeding grounds of red and fallow deer, wild ox, mountain sheep and goats.

As soon as the ice had gone and the valleys had become clothed with vegetation, a hunting and food-gathering race of people wandered northwards from South Western Europe round about 8000-6000 BC. They are known as *Mesolithic* or *Middle Stone Age* men. They came over to England by the land bridge which still connected this island with the Continent. Proof of their appearance has been recognised by the finding of "pigmy-flint" tools or microliths on dry open sites upon the higher slopes. The people who fashioned them were nomads, and followed the "trods" of the wild ox and deer, which they slew with arrows and spears tipped with sharpened flint points. They also shaped bones and deer antlers into fish-hooks and harpoons, and made primitive saws by inserting rows of flint flakes into suitable lengths of wood or bone. Agriculture and the domestication of animals were unknown to them. They were continually on the move, exploring the Pennines during the summer months only. They lived upon the flesh of animals, birds and fishes, fungi, berries and hazel nuts. Their camps were rough shelters of branches or leaves covering shallow holes in the ground. No traces of these remain, but there is evidence that they made periodical visits to Swaledale. Microlithic flints have been picked up upon the hill-tops where the peat has been eroded by wind and water.

Mesolithic men were superseded round about 2500 BC by the *Neolithic* or *New Stone Age men.* Britain was now an island, from about 5000 BC., and they crossed from western Europe in skin-covered or dug-out canoes. They were taller than their predecessors and had a primitive knowledge of farming. Those few who came into Swaledale, like their Old Stone Age ancestors, were still hunters but may have herded the wild oxen and sheep which they found there. These animals became domesticated and supplied milk as well as flesh for their owners. The tools used by the New Stone Age men were fashioned from flint and stone and were larger and more finished than those of Mesolithic people. A fragment of a Neolithic axe-head was found near Muker. It is composed of volcanic ash stone. It is beauti-fully smooth, and was probably fixed and bound with thongs to a cleft stick or shaft, and used for cutting trees and branches. We know where the axe-head was actually quarried and shaped. There is a crag on the side of Pike o' Stickle in Langdale where the remains of partly fashioned tools and throw-aways have been picked up. The Muker axe-head find suggests that as Neolithic men moved eastwards over the Pennines, they brought their tools with them, or there may have been a trade or barter in these implements from their factories in the Lake District. Two axe-heads were also found at Healaugh. One of their leaf-arrowheads was picked up upon the slopes of Calver and a "petit tranchet" type of arrowhead upon Grinton moor.

More sophisticated tribes came into Swaledale called "Beaker" folk, arriving about 1900-1800 BC. They were so-named because they made a distinctive type of pot or beaker. They were the first of the *Bronze Age* invaders. They still used flint implements, which they perfected to a fine degree. They also kept domestic animals and exercised a form of primitive agriculture. Traces of their settlements are found in Swaledale and they may have lived permanently there, having given up a nomadic way of life.

It is considered that the "Beaker" folk were responsible for making the earthwork known as Maiden Castle on Harkerside, 1¼ miles south west of Grinton. Dr. Whitaker noticed it nearly 150 years ago. He thought it was an encampment or defensive work, but the way in which the interior is commanded from the hill above points against this theory. If the men of that period were choosing a camp site they would have preferred a prominence like Harker Hill, or Calver Hill on the opposite side of the valley, with its outlook along the length of Swaledale and Arkengarthdale. Present day opinion suggests that Maiden Castle is a modest counterpart to the first phase of Stonehenge, and may have been used as a place of religious ritual and human sacrifice, or a place of assembly for feasting and other social purposes. However crude it looks today, it was fashioned out of a very unpromising site and must have been a colossal undertaking for the few able-bodied men and women who were available in this sparsely populated area. A ditch originally 10-15 feet deep, with its bank thrown inwards, covers an area of 1¾ acres. It is nearly circular in shape, about 300 feet in diameter, and entered from the east by an avenue of piled stones 120 yards in length. At the entrance to the avenue is a round barrow, which has been damaged by someone, so the story goes, searching for a non-existent treasure. There are traces of 2 or 3 hut circles in the south east corner and one near the north east. The date of Maiden Castle is estimated at between 1600 and 1000 BC.

Barbed and tanged arrow-heads of flint have been picked up in many parts of the dale. They are usually found high up on the slopes. One lay amongst gritstone pebbles where the peat had been washed away, near Keld Springs above Bloody Vale. Another was found on the surface of a rough track leading to the hillside from Lodge Green and several others upon the slopes of Calver Hill. The flint used in their manufacture must have been imported to the district. The nearest places where flint is found in its natural state are the chalk wolds of the East Riding or Flamborough Head so Swaledale man had communication with his brethren in the larger settlements of those areas.

Between 1500 and 1000 BC further Bronze Age tribes reached our coasts. Although a certain amount of killing may have occurred as the tribes in possession defended their properties, there was probably a great deal of inter-marriage, and the earlier invaders would have been absorbed by those who came later. These various tribes were, after all, of the same ethnic culture, originating in the Mediterranean countries.

To what extent the inhabitants of Swaledale were affected by these periodical migrations, we do not know. The first groups to settle in Swaledale, although from a race which practised agriculture, probably existed almost entirely by hunting and fishing. Cultivation was difficult, because the flat land by the river was still swamp and marsh, and the hillsides were covered with forest. Unlike the chalk hills of the East Riding, the moorland was unsuitable for the growing of grain crops, although the finding of a "saddle" quern near Healaugh suggests that some kind of corn was grown in the dale.

How a chance happening can reveal to us something of the past is worth relating. About 50 years ago, a well-known gamekeeper went rabbiting but lost his ferret in a heap of rocks and scree lying upon an undercliff below Arngill Scar near West Arngill. Trying to get at the ferret, he started removing the stones. It was a hard task. Having excavated the heap to a depth of 4 feet, he brought to light a pile of human bones. He took away part of the jaw bone and carefully replaced the bones and stones as he had found them. He finally erected a small cairn on top to mark the site. The gamekeeper died many years ago, but in 1956 his son, having remembered the incident, suggested that a further investigation should be made. A party of about half a dozen people climbed up the steep hillside to the site. The cairn was still there, and after clearing away the stones the heap of bones was discovered. They comprised the remaining part of the jaw-bone, eye sockets, frontal bones and about one third of the brain case, together with a number of limb bones, ribs and vertebrae.

Parts of the brain case, the jaw and some ox teeth found on the site, were submitted to Dr. Oakley's Department at the Kensington Natural History Museum, who wrote to say that they were 2000 - 3000 years old. This dating would be well within the Bronze Age period. The bones were nearly all broken, suggesting that inhumation took place some months after death, when the flesh had been removed either by decay or other means. They were then thrown into a rock crevasse and covered with a heap of stones.

There are few authenticated records of the finding of implements or weapons of bronze. Up to date, evidences of Bronze Age men, have been finely cut arrow-heads, three or four tool-making sites, a flanged bronze axe found near Reeth (York Museum), a few round barrows and hut circles, and the Arngill skeleton.

About 400-300 BC a series of *Iron Age* tribes crossed the Channel and North Sea. The Brigantes, a federation of Celtic tribes from Central Europe, eventually established themselves from the East Coast of Yorkshire to the Irish Sea and as far North as the Solway Firth. They were familiar with iron working but as iron deteriorates very quickly few of their metal implements have survived, as have the arrows and tools of flint and stone made by earlier people. They still used stone hammers, however, with perforated holes into which were fitted wooden shafts. In the York Museum there is a perforated battle-axe found in Arkengarthdale.

Traces of enclosures, hut circles and burial mounds on Harker-side and Iveletside may belong to the Iron Age people. Upon the western slopes of Calver Hill are the remains of a cattle enclosure. It is 200 feet in diameter and lies to the East of Cringley Hill. The latter name is derived from the Norse word "KRINGLA" meaning a circle. It is interesting to speculate whether or not the hill was called Cringley or Kringla by the later Scandinavian settlers because of the circular enclosure which they found nearby. There are other and smaller enclosures visible in the same vicinity.

The Brigantes were not easily subdued by the Roman conquerors and they retreated to the fastnesses of the hills and fells where they built themselves hill-top forts.

Archaeologists have for a long time been intrigued by the deep embankments and ditches dug just under the brow of the eastern side of High Harker Hill. These seem to continue northwards in the Reeth direction until they reach the downward slope. Then there is a break of 1000 yards and an embankment appears again, ending almost at the edge of the river Swale. Another similar earthwork runs parallel to this lower one and also ends near the Swale, but it can be picked up again on the north side of the river near Fremington. It then runs up through that village and finally ends one third of the way up to Fremington Edge.

The portion which follows the brow of High Harker Hill suggests that this eminence was intended to be used as a hill-fort by the Brigantes, possibly after their defeat by the Romans at Stanwick near Gilling about AD 71-74. The dyke, which embodies in its alignment 350 yards of scar and scree, has its bank thrown up on the higher side of the ditch, suggesting that it is a defence against people advancing up the slope. The north and north-west sides of High Harker Hill have steep natural scars and on the remaining south-east edge are signs of a continuance of the dyke. Up to date, no traces of habitations such as hut circles or cattle enclosures have been found on the flat summit of the hill. Perhaps, as happened at Stanwick, the Romans surprised and drove the defenders away before the fort was finished. Stanwick was a hastily built fort 850 acres in area built near Gilling, in an attempt to halt the Roman legions.

The most complete Iron Age site lies near Richmond, between Whitcliffe woods and High Applegarth, just under Willance's Leap. It consists of two or three large square cattle enclosures protected by a high cliff to the North and a substantial rampart to the South. At the entrance to one of the enclosures are the remains of a hut dwelling with two chambers, one leading into the other. The Royal Commission for Historical Monuments has surveyed the site and considers that it was occupied by an Iron Age group up to 600 AD.,

13

150 years after the Romans had left Britain.

One can also see the remains of a moraine near Low Whita Bridge, called Howe Hill, which has been fortified in what might well have been Iron Age times. It has a ditch on three sides and the fourth side drops steeply down to the River Swale.

The Romans in Swaledale

RECORDS OF Roman antiquities, not all confirmed, found in Reeth, Fremington and district have been noted in guide and topographical books. These include fragments of pottery found at Reeth; bronze horse-harness at Fremington Hagg (York Museum Handbook); a coin found in the entrenchment below Fremington Edge (York Museum 1895); and a pig of lead inscribed with the name "HADRIAN" at Hurst.[1] (Hadrian reigned 117-138 AD.) Another pig of lead was found in Crackpot Gill on which, according to Mr. Francis Garth who found it, were imprinted a Roman emperor's head and some lettering. His daughter told me that her father melted down the pig of lead "to fix iron crooks into stone gateposts".

The Romans, as we know, were familiar with the mining and smelting of lead, copper, iron and tin, so that they were quite capable of finding the rich lead deposits at Hurst. Whether slave labour from the ranks of the defeated Brigantes was used to mine the ore, or whether, as is more likely, the local inhabitants co-operated and fattened on the Roman occupation is a matter for debate. I think that we can assume that the Iron Age tribes, when once they were subdued, lived peacefully alongside the Roman colonizers, as they did in many parts of Northern Britain.

There are two mounds in the valley bottom below Grinton Bridge which are the remains of the moraine after the Swale had broken through.. One has a square platform upon it and the other is surrounded by a bank. These may have been fortified in Roman times.

Mr. Brian Hartley of Leeds University has stated that the Romans occupied a fortlet at Reeth: Reeth lies roughly midway between Bowes and Catterick, and between Bowes and Bainbridge, all three being the sites of Roman forts. Another bit of evidence was supplied by Mr. R. Chapman of Bainbridge. He discovered in some medieval records, that the road passing over Summer Lodge and Whitaside moors from Bainbridge, via Askrigg to Reeth, was called "Waingate"[2] meaning waggon road. At that time the only roads which were suitable for wheeled traffic were roads of Roman construction. This supports Mr. Hartley's theory that a Roman fortlet existed at Reeth.

(1) The present whereabouts of this pig of lead is unknown.

(2) called Windgate on the 2½" ordnance map

The Norsemen Settle in the Dale

AFTER THE ROMANS left Britain about 450 AD., the history of Swaledale became a closed book for nearly 600 years. The area west of Reeth was a "chase" or "deer forest" where the Anglo-Saxon and Danish chieftains hunted game. It formed part of a larger area embracing the Arkengarthdale and New Forests [1] and the Wensleydale Forest. We know that the district was the haunt of wild deer, bear, boar and wolves. In fact wolves were hunted there until 1369 AD., and red-deer as late as the seventeenth century. Its occupation by man was probably limited to forest wardens and game watchers, and odd settlements of the descendants of the earlier Iron Age inhabitants. It was not until the end of the tenth century that the upper dale attracted the land-hungry Norsemen, who had been occupying northern Ireland and the Isle of Man for some decades.

Evidence that they occupied Upper Swaledale is borne out by the fact that many of the place-names and geographical features are Old Norse in origin. For instance, the old Norse word "saetr", meaning a "shieling or hill pasture", is undoubtedly the second element of various place names. The most obvious of these is Ravenseat — "Hrafn's saetr", and Gunnerside [2] "Gunnarr's saetr", the first element in both cases being personal names. In the same way we get Harkerside, Rogan's Seat, Hugh Seat and Luna Seat.[3] Keld is derived from "kelda" — a spring; Muker from "mior" — narrow, "akr" — a field; and Arkengarthdale was "the valley of Arkil's enclosure". The Old Norse "dalr" — a dale or valley, is commonplace. The foregoing are only a few examples of old Norse place-names.

Even the dalesman's dialect speech bears a strong resemblance to this ancient language. Unfortunately it is now becoming almost forgotten except by a few of the older generation.

When we get down to Healaugh, Reeth and Grinton the names suddenly change and become Anglo-Saxon in character. We then have the "tun" (or "ton") names meaning "enclosure" or "village", such as Fremington — the village of *Fremi's* people"; Grinton — "green *tun*"; and Ellerton — "alder tun".

The Anglo-Saxon influence in the lower part of Swaledale is

evident from the cultivation terraces or "lynchets" which they have left behind, traces of these are very noticeable to the north west of Reeth and at Marrick, Marske and Downholme.

(1) The New Forest covered the large tract of moorland to the east of Arkengarthdale towards Barningham and Ravensworth.

(2) Gunnerside is still referred to as "Gunnersitt".

(3) marked on the map as "Lovely Seat"

Next Came the Normans

THE NORSEMEN had not long been settled in Upper Swaledale, when Britain was successfully invaded by the Normans. Whatever else the conquerors accomplished, they established a uniform system of land control in the north of England. William I realized that if the rebellious native tribes were to be pacified and at the same time his gains defended against the marauding Scots, the establishment of strong defensive bases would be essential. He ordered castles to be built in many places and rewarded his more trusty supporters with large slices of territory. He gave to his kinsman, Count Alan Rufus, an area stretching eastwards from the Pennines, to include the whole of the North Riding of Yorkshire. It was known as the Honour of Richmond. Count Alan was a Breton and he, in turn, gave portions of his territory to his Breton knights, subject to "suite and service" in times of war.

Count Alan probably built Richmond Castle. The town itself grew around this strongly-built fortress where lived some of the descendants of his French-Breton soldiers of occupation. The large open market square and the names of some of the narrow streets suggest a strong influence from across the Channel. Count Stephen of Brittany was Alan's successor and when Walter de Gant, a Norman knight, married Matilda, Stephen's daughter, he received with her a grant of the whole of Swaledale.

The Gant family were lords of Upper Swaledale for some time. In 1125, or thereabouts, Matilda, the wife of Walter, granted to Bridlington Priory "the church of St. Andrew in Swaledale with Grinton and all its vicinity." This came from her marriage portion with her husband's consent. Walter de Gant was the actual founder of the Priory in the reign of Henry I. Walter de Gant was succeeded by his son Gilbert, Earl of Lincoln, whose only child, Alice, died without issue. Alice, following her grandmother's example, some time before 1174 left in her will to Bridlington Priory —

"... all the pasture and herbage of Swaledale from Herkey (Harkerside) as far as the stream of Harwardesdale (Haverdale or Crackpot gill) as it lies on the south side of the River Swale, upwards towards the south as far as my land extends; and of my wood as much as is needed for making houses and folds for cattle; reserving my wild beasts. Moreover I have quitclaimed to the same canons whatever assarts [1] they have made in my forest since the death of Walter de Gaunt."

Robert de Gant, Alice's uncle, who next inherited the manor, confirmed this grant in 1185-91, and also enlarged upon the privileges given. Licence was given to the Priory to make hay, take what wood they needed without felling trees, make houses and folds for their two "vaccaries" [2] and enough wattles to make two houses. Two dogs were allowed at each vaccary, to be loose at night and tied up by day.

A strange episode occurred at the turn of the thirteenth century. The Augustinian Prior of Bridlington made a complaint which evidently reached Pope Innocent III (1198-1216) reporting that the Archdeacon of Richmond, in making a visitation to his Archdeaconry, came to Grinton church "with 97 horses, 21 dogs and 3 hawks, and, in a brief hour, consumed more than would have maintained their house for a considerable period". This led to a mandate from the Pope commanding that, in making visitations, nothing more should be exacted than the statutes of the Lateran Council permit, etc.

In 1241-2, another Gilbert de Gant whose head manor was at Healaugh granted to the monks of Rievaulx Abbey —

"all the pasture of Swaledale with its appurtenances (west of Whitsundale Beck, the Swale and Oxnop Beck), to have there their cattle of what number and kind they wish ..... and folds, and lodges for their cattle, and dogs and horns and to make hay and enclose meadows ... and to have houses for the brothers and their servants ... and to take the wood of the said Gilbert within the stated boundaries as much as they need for houses, fences, hearths, folds and lodges ... and to cut the branches of trees to feed their cattle ... and to kill wolves by whatever means they can, and to pass and repass freely with their cattle to the stated pasture through all the lands of the said Gilbert and his heirs except through cornfields and meadows. So that no one else may have any cattle in the same pasture except the said monks."

So, with the exception of that portion of the Healaugh manor lying between Whitsundale Beck and the manor of Fremington, on the north side of the Swale; and between Haverdale Beck and Oxnop Beck; Upper Swaledale appears to have been controlled by religious orders. As for the lower part of Swaledale, Marrick Priory, founded in Henry II's reign, held lands granted to it by Roger of Aske, and Ellerton

Priory, founded about the same time, held lands further east.

(1) clearings in the forest

(2) grazing-farms

Swaledale Surnames from the Lay Subsidy Rolls

THE LAY SUBSIDY was a kind of "capital levy" imposed by Edward I and other English kings to enable them to continue their campaigns against the Scots, and for other military adventures in Europe. One of these levies was made in 1301. The individual's assessment was one-fifteenth of the value of his moveable goods such as draught animals, cows, sheep, lambs, grain, peas and beans. Household goods, farming tools, seeds and poultry were probably exempt. The levy ranged from a few pence to about twelve shillings per farmstead, and it would appear that hardly anyone escaped the tax.

In the 1301 Subsidy Rolls are given the names of the Swaledale tax-payers. Probably very few people living in the dale owned inherited surnames. People were almost illiterate. Indeed until the tax-gatherer came along there was no need to distinguish between the various bearers of the Christian names, the most common of which were William, John, Robert, Thomas, Simon, Stephen, Geoffrey, Roger and Richard. These were all English versions of Norman-French names which at that time had displaced in popularity the pure Saxon and Scandinavian names of an earlier period.

Amongst themselves the inhabitants would avoid confusion by giving one another "nick-names", some of which were destined to become permanent surnames. It was customary to give "by-names" to one's neighbours until recent times, in fact the custom still goes on in some villages. The clerk who compiled the subsidy list was compelled to identify and particularize each individual to satisfy the exchequer that all were paying their dues. A great number had already been given place-names and topographical names, i.e. the name of the village in which they lived or from whence they came, or the particular spot at which their farmsteads were situated. Then came occupational, personal and finally nick-names.

The inhabitants named in the Lay Subsidy Rolls are given in capitals. Of the place names, there are still BLADES and KEARTONS living in the dale. The Subsidy Rolls also give Robert de RAYNSATE (Ravenseat), Roger de SATEROM (Satron), John de GUNNERSETE

(Gunnerside), Sibilla de CRAKEPOT (Crackpot), Simon de OYNEHOP (Oxnop), William de RYTHE (Reeth), William de FREMINGTON and Stephen de HAVERDALE. Jordan of Kearton has an unusual Christian name though it was fairly common in the fourteenth century. P.H. Reaney in his "Dictionary of British Surnames" (whom I freely quote) says that "the name of the river Jordan was used as a Christian name by returning crusaders who brought back with them Jordan water for the baptism of their children."

The topographical names include del WRA, "a dweller in a nook or corner." This may be one of the origins of the surnames of RAW or WRAY. Raw is still a common Swaledale name and Wray appears in the Grinton Parish registers between 1650 and 1700. The names given to Robert ATTEBECK (Beck), Thomas UNDERHOU (Underhill), Bernard del BANCK (Bank), Henry WODE (Wood), William BRADRIGG (Broderick) — "a dweller on the broad ridge", and Thomas del DYKE are familiar today. Broderick is the name of a very ancient Dales family and the early variant of Bradrigg may have become permanent by 1301. Thomas of the DYKE probably had a farmstead adjoining the pre-historic dikes on Harkerside already mentioned. There exists today a farm named Dike House on this particular site.

Many of the occupational names are still in use. REEVE was the bailiff and had oversight of the game. Robert the CLERIC (Clarke) was a parson or a man in a religious order. Alan BELLE may have rung the bell for service (or perhaps he was the son of Isabel). WARD, a watchman, and MILLER or MILNER are still common Dales names. WEAVER and FULLER are descriptive of processes in cloth-making, and CARPENTER, CARTER and SMITH are all occupational names.

MAN was a servant or one who owed feudal service. Richard OYSEL's name may have been a shortening of the Old French "Oiseleur" — a bird catcher or fowler, or even a falconer. Simon PEGGE was "a maker or seller of pegs" (or from Margaret).

The personal names, Robert son of STEPHEN, William GODFREY, Lora the wife of GILBERT, Robert son of WARINE (from which we get Waring and Wharin) are in modern use as surnames. COLLAN is likely to be a variant of "Colin" or "Collin", a pet-name of Nicholas.

Nearly all the nick-names have their modern equivalents. LONG needs no explanation. PESECODDE (Pescodd) was Old English for "pea bag". TODDE (Todd) meant "crafty", "fox-like" from Mediaeval English "tod" — a fox. FOX meant the same. STURDY was "impetuously brave" and SCHACKLOCK (Shakelock) had the habit of shaking back his long hair. KYNGE was a nick-name given to someone with kingly qualities or who had taken part as a king in some pageant or "mystery play". FROST may have had a cold manner or distant personal approach, or, perhaps, was "white-haired". FREEMAN was no longer a "villein" and was free from compulsory labour to the lord of the manor. PRATY has probably come down to us as Pratt meaning "astute, cunning". SHAKE may be derived from the Old Norse personal name "Skeggi", meaning "bearded". DYL exists as the modern surname Dill. SUDDE just means "South", given to a person coming from that direction.

There is also a miscellaneous collection of names such as NEWETRUITE, SPIRTING, BLAHAT, CROBE, HAUDEX, and TETTY which have fascinating possibilities and which the reference books fail to elucidate.

Many of these names died out during the centuries, due to change or perhaps to a lack of male heirs but also to plagues and epidemics which in those days were ever recurrent. Only fifty years after these names were recorded in the Subsidy Rolls occurred the "Black Death", a plague which ravaged Europe and is said to have carried off over one quarter of the population, although it may have been less deadly in isolated districts such as Swaledale.

Marrick Priory

MARRICK PRIORY was founded by Roger de Aske in the reign of Henry II (1154-89) for Benedictine Nuns. The original charter has been lost or destroyed. Thus records of the priory are very meagre. Even the exact date of the foundation is obscure. It is thought by some that it could not have been built earlier than 1165 because the original grant by Roger de Aske was made with the consent of Conan, Earl of Richmond, who did not become seised of the Earldom until that date.

The priory received visitations from the Archbishop of York and the Archdeacon of Richmond from time to time, as did other monasteries in Richmondshire. One such visitation occurred on Tuesday before the feast of St. Denis, 1252, after which certain "articles" or rules were sent for the observance of the nuns. These may have been the usual instructions issued to nunneries by the Benedictine Order.

The prioress was directed to be affable to her nuns and to treat them kindly. Their faults were to be corrected privately in chapter, and equal punishments made for equal guilt. Leave from the abbey was given only in special circumstances such as the sickness of friends or other worthy reasons, and then only if accompanied by a "prudent and mature nun". The time for return was fixed, non-compliance with which was subject to a severe penalty. In order that their minds did not become pre-occupied with worldly matters, the nuns were prohibited from sitting with guests outside the cloister after curfew had sounded at eight o'clock, unless the guests had arrived so late that it was impossible to entertain them earlier. In any case a nun should not remain alone with a guest, but others should be present. The priory's means were very modest. Guests were therefore discouraged from staying more than one night. No one was admitted to the house except by bishop's licence. If this rule was broken the visitors concerned would be expelled "without hope of mercy". Similarly the prioress would be deposed, and any nuns conniving would be made to fast on bread and water for two months, except on Sundays and festivals. Special licences were necessary before girls or women could be accepted into the convent as boarders. Serving women might however be employed therein to do such work as it was indecorous for the nuns or sisters to perform.

None of the provisions supplied for the maintenance of the nuns were to be sold without consent of the master or steward of the priory. Lists of the oxen, cows, horses and stock were to be inscribed on two rolls, one remaining at the convent and the other with the master. The latter's duties were to conduct the priory's business with the outside world and the guardianship of the "granges" (farms) so that everything was in order when a visitation took place. On Maundy Thursdays, alms were distributed to the poor at the gates of the monastery to the value of sixteen shillings and eight-pence. Various other benefactions were made during the year, amounting to nine pounds, four shillings and eightpence halfpenny, a large sum for such a small convent.

This glimpse into the life of Marrick Priory is all that history can tell us. At the Dissolution of the Monasteries in 1539, it was surrendered by the prioress, Christabella Cowper and sixteen nuns. The prioress received an annual pension of one hundred shillings and the nuns amounts varying between sixty-six shillings and eightpence and twenty shillings.

A list of the prioresses is given below:-

Agnes	occurs	1200
Isabel Surrais	occurs	1250-1263
Alina	occurs	1280
Margaret	occurs	1282
Alice de Helperby	occurs	1293
Juliana	occurs	1298
Margaret	occurs	1321 and 1327
Elizabeth de Berden	occurs	1326 and 1333
Elizabeth	occurs	1352
Maud de Melsonby	occurs	1376
Elizabeth	occurs	1391
Agnes	occurs	1400-1413
Alice de Ravenswathe	occurs	1433 and 1449
Cecilia Metcalf	occurs	1464 and 1498 (died 1502)
Agnes Wenslawe	occurs	1502 (died 1510)
Isabella Berningham	occurs	1511 (died 1511)
Christabella Cowper	occurs	1530

In 1545-6, after the Dissolution, Marrick priory was granted to John Uvedale, and included in the grant was "the spyttelhouse de

Stanemore in Stanemore". This hospital or spittal formerly belonged to the priory.

The present church of St. Andrew was built in 1811. It was constructed out of the remains of the old priory church and bits of arches, piers and lancet windows can be found in the newer edifice. There still stand the walls of the former chancel outside the church.

Uvedale or other successive owners of the priory site created a farmstead just south of the church, also using stone from the priory buildings. It is said that the farm livingroom incorporated in its construction part of the nuns' refectory. There is a frieze of carving over what was once the old firestead, and some of the walls are six feet in thickness.

Marrick priory stands upon a bluff, high above the left bank of the River Swale; a gated road leads to the ruins. This branches off the Fremington-Marske road about one mile from the former village. It can also be approached by descending the three hundred and sixty-five steps from Marrick village, through picturesque woodland.

Upon the opposite bank of the Swale is a very ancient track which follows the east side of a still older entrenchment. The track has the appearance of a sunken lane which leaves the main Richmond road fifty yards east of the old toll-bar cottage. The lane divides as it nears the river, one part going to the left and reaching the river at the Abbey ford just under the priory. The other portion continues down to the river where there are stepping-stones. These can be easily crossed in dry weather and lead to a footpath to Marrick village.

Ellerton Priory

ELLERTON PRIORY was a convent of Cistercian nuns. Leland called it "a priori of white clothed nunnes, stonding in a valle ..... a mile beneth marik priory". The date of its foundation is ambiguous. Some say it was created by Warner, the chief steward of the Earl of Richmond, others think that it was founded by Warner's son, Wymar, during the reign of Henry II. Speight[1] relates that, during excavations at the site of the priory, a stone coffin lid was discovered, upon which was inscribed "Hic jacet Wimerus" which seems to infer that Wymar was the founder and was buried there. The first recorded prioress was Alice (1227). In that year she was involved in a law-suit respecting the church of Whixley, brought against her by the prior of Kirkham. The finding is unknown but the dispute was renewed the following year at Westminster.

It is recorded that in 1286 Adam of Ellerton held a freehold messuage of the priory and a carucate[2] of land in Ellerton. Ellen, who was prioress at that time, claimed from him, in exchange,

"... a yearly payment of nine pence for fine of wapentake and county courts and four pence for ward of Richmond Castle[3] and that he give relief and do homage and suit at her court at Ellerton every three weeks, and should make for the said prioress and convent and her household one entertainment (convivium) yearly for one day, and that he should ride with her in place of seneschal[4] and that he should find a horse for her, at his own cost, as often as she should journey."

Adam evidently considered that this was asking too much and it was finally settled that —

"Adam undertakes that he and his heirs will do suit every three weeks, pay 13d yearly, render yearly 3 lb of wax at the octave of the feast of St. Peter *ad Vincula*[5] and will do homage on the death of himself and his heirs." (sic)

In 1274 the priory had some trouble with one of the sisters, Maud daughter of Roger de Hunmanby, details of which remain unknown. She was excommunicated by Archbishop Giffard who reported his action to the justices of the King's Bench, and complained that she was obdurate and persisted in contumacy and offence, that she was "contemning the keys of the Church". He asked the justices to shun her and repel her by every legitimate means until she came back to him, seeking benefit of absolution.

The priory was said to be one of the humblest of all monastic foundations. It possessed two bovates of land at Ellerton in 1287 and the prioress was the joint owner with Thomas de Hereford of the manor of Ellerton cum Stainton. When the Scots made one of their raids into Swaledale in 1347, they violated the priory and stole or destroyed its charters and writings.

At the dissolution, the income of the priory, totalling fourteen pounds, fourteen shillings and eightpence, came from rents etc., in Barforth, Barton, Melsonby, Richmond, Studdow and Walburn, these being gifts of land from various benefactors. The value of the priory site with gardens, mills, meadows,and glebe was one pound. After deducting outgoings of four shillings and twopence, there was a nett balance of fifteen pounds, ten shillings and sixpence.

The following is a list of some of the prioresses taken from various sources:-

Alice	occurs	1227
Petronilla	occurs	1251
Ellen	occurs	1268
Sibil	occurs	1299
Margaret	occurs	1347
Mary Gray	date uncertain	
Alice Sherwood	occurs	1429

Joan, who surrendered the priory in 1537

All that remains of Ellerton priory is a west tower, with a round arch to the nave and something of the walls. In the nave are three or four carved stones lying half-buried in the debris. It lies about a mile to the east of Marrick priory upon the south side of the River Swale. After the Dissolution the site was demised to one Ralph Closeby and in 1601 came into possession of the Drax family, the present owners.

(1) see "Romantic Richmondshire" (1897).

(2) a measure of land, as much as can be tilled with one plough in a season.

(3) for protection from the inroads of the Scots.

(4) steward or major-domo.

(5) on Lammas day, the "loaf mass", Aug. 1st.

The Swales of Swale Hall

DESCENDED FROM the Gant family, mentioned in an earlier chapter, was one Alured de Swale. He was a nephew of Walter de Gant who was granted the lordship of Swaledale through a lucky marriage with the daughter of Count Stephen of Brittany, Earl of Richmond. Walter in his turn gave to his nephew, Alured, West Grinton and other lands belonging to the town of Reeth. There seems to be some doubt as to where the boundaries of these lands extended and whether they conflicted with the grant made by the Gant family to Bridlington Priory of "the Church of St. Andrew in Swaledale with Grinton and all its vicinity." Nevertheless the Swale family lived here upwards of five centuries.

Alured de Swale fought at the Battle of the Standard[1]. His grandson William died during a pilgrimage to Jerusalem in one of the crusades. Another descendant, Robert, was returned by the Sheriff of Yorkshire in the reign of Edward II, as one of the lords of the township of Grinton held conjointly with the Prior of Bridlington.

William over Swale owned land in Reeth in 1273-4 and paid his "subsidy" and took part in the Scottish wars. One branch of the family acquired the manor of South Stainley and had numerous descendants. John Swale became a mounted archer at the battle of Agincourt and his son, William, during the reign of Henry VI (1422-1461), built Swale Hall, which lies a quarter mile west of Grinton church.

Another member of the family known as "Old Solomon Swale" of Swale Hall, along with his brother Richard, was for a long time a prisoner in York Castle, for a debt which he did not owe. Before he died in great poverty Solomon sold Swale Hall to his kinsman, another Solomon Swale of South Stainley, thus merging the two manors in one ownership. This Solomon[2] was a barrister of Grays Inn and in the time of Charles I was a Member of Parliament for the "rotten borough" of Aldborough, near Boroughbridge. He proposed in Parliament the restoration of Charles II on the 17th May, 1660, and in consideration of his loyalty he was created a baronet in the following June. In addition he received a gift of two thousand pounds in 1668 and a loan of two thousand pounds to be repaid in twenty years. His eldest son Henry inherited his title, and became the second baronet.

The third baronet was also called Solomon. He got involved in several Chancery suits touching upon lead-mines on Harkerside. These were decided against him. But worse was to follow. A retired clerk in the Exchequer Office, Reginald Marriott, having discovered that the Swale family had neglected to renew for many years their Crown lease of Swale Hall, procured by petition to the Lords of the Treasury, in the name of George Tushingham, the lease of a greater part of the estate to himself. Sir Solomon beggared himself with more lawsuits for its recovery and in the end was thrown into the Fleet prison, where he died of a broken heart in 1733. As he had no issue the title passed to his nephew, Sir Sebastian Swale, fourth baronet, a merchant of Malaga in Spain. When the latter died, having only three daughters, the title became extinct but it was revived by another Swale in the late nineteenth century. Swale Hall was sold in 1786 and became a farm.

Most members of the Swale family retained the old faith after the Reformation and were often fined and their possessions confiscated. "Old" Solomon Swale and his wife Ann were cited as Catholic recusants in 1615 and had suffered from fines for the previous ten years. Grinton parish had a high percentage of Catholics who refused to participate in Anglican communion services. In a survey made in 1604, there were seventy recusants living in the parish, all of whom were liable to fines of two shillings a week so long as they stayed away from church.

---

(1) 1138 AD – three miles north of Northallerton.
(2) died 1678 age seventy.

The Ancient Custom of Tenant Rights

IN AN EARLIER CHAPTER, mention is made of the Gaunt family who were granted the whole of Swaledale by William the Conqueror's vassal, Count Stephen of Richmond. They introduced to the dale a feudal system of tenure which continued for two or three centuries. A manorial survey of 1274, upon the death of Gilbert de Gaunt (the third of that name) describes this system of land tenure. The Gaunt demesne lands included a manor house at Healaugh with 100 acres of arable land; 27½ acres of meadow at Fytum (Feetham) and Skaleflat (? Scale Ings); and also vaccaries and pastures of the forest.

There were also 9 cottars or villeins holding 24 bovates[1] in exchange for their servile labour on the lord's demesne lands. In addition there were a further 32 cottars with small holdings totalling 51 acres of arable land and one rood with tofts[2] in Healaugh. These cottars were also liable for the same labour services and were nominally serfs who provided free labour at the order of the lord (or of his steward). They had to till his land, shepherd his sheep and supply him with peat and coal for the heating of his manor house.

At a slightly higher social level were the tenants-at-will, i.e. the holders of tenancies restricted to the whims and rules of the landlord. These included 4 tenants at Ruckroft (Rawcroft) with 23½ acres and 4 tofts, and 9 tenants in Arklegarth (Arkengarthdale) with 29 acres of meadow and 9 tofts. Higher still in the social hierarchy were the free tenants: Hugh, son of Henry, who held the village of Fremington "by the services of one-fourth part of a knight's fee" and one sporting dog yearly; William Overswale holding one carucate of land, one assart and 1½ bovates in Reeth, subject to military service and a yearly rent; John of Reeth, John Ode and William of Dalton, tenants owing similar services. The last-named, in addition to rent, was liable to pay one pound of "cumin"[3] annually.

Finally there were the two religious houses, Bridlington Priory holding the town of Grinton with its church, and Rievaulx Abbey holding the "vill called Meuhaker" (Muker).

During the 14th century, this servile feudal system began to relax to the advantage of the peasants. The Black Death (1348-49), which according to some estimates carried off one quarter of the population of the country, created a tremendous shortage of labour. Those cottars and villeins who previously were compelled to give their labours free were now able to demand payment   for their hire, and to hold their modest cottages and allotments by paying money rents.

From this beginning developed very gradually a system of tenant rights. Each tenant worked his fields without interference from the lord of the manor, subject to certain fixed fines and rents, and to liability for military service in time of war.[4] To begin with, there were no written agreements or leasehold documents, because neither side was sufficiently literate. But later on, a tenant was able to hold his lands on what became known as a "copy-hold" tenure, and to receive a written copy of the details of his tenancy as inscribed upon the manorial rolls.

As time passed, new lords took over the manors. The religious houses lost their possessions to the Crown and their estates were sold or granted to newcomers as part payment for their services to the reigning monarchs. When the Wharton family became possessed of the greater part of Upper Swaledale, Muker and the confiscated Rievaulx Abbey properties became a separate manor. The local inhabitants had enjoyed certain privileges and customs and had always held their tenements subject to a total annual payment or yearly rental of £48=13=4.This was payable on "the next Sunday after the feast of St. Andrew, the Apostle, at, or within, the Chapel of Mewacre" (Muker).

Additional duties and customs however were imposed, as landlord succeeded landlord. In 1618, the tenants of Muker petitioned Philip, the third Lord Wharton, to settle for ever the ancient custom of tenant's rights. To this purpose an indenture was made in that year between Philip Lord Wharton and Sir Thomas Wharton, his son, on the one hand, and Ralph Alderson, William Harkey, John Milner, Alexander, James and William Metcalfe, representing the tenants, on the other hand. This document finally fixed the various fines and duties as follows:- each tenant paid one penny, 'commonly called a Godspenny" upon a change of the lord of the manor. Upon alienation of his copyhold tenement, (i.e. if it was passed on to some other person), the new tenant was liable to pay a 20 years fine, but if the tenant was one of his children, a 10 years fine only was payable. The amount of the fine was 20(or 10) times the annual rent. As an example, if a copy-hold farm rented at 6s=8d per annum was alienated, the incoming tenant would pay a fine of £6=13=4 in addition to his annual rent.

Added to this, he was subjected to a Running Fine or Gressom. This meant that at the end of the first 5 years he paid a fine equal to half the amount of his annual rent. This represented 3s=4d in the case of the example just quoted. At the end of the next 5 years he paid one quarter of the rent, namely 1s=8d. These alternating payments would be continued during all the time of his tenancy. The lord of the manor agreed that he would not interfere with any enclosing of common pastures which the tenants might undertake, provided that such enclosing had the consent of the majority of the tenants; neither would he claim any additional rent or fines for such actions. This new tenancy agreement was made in consideration of a sum of £1654=13=4 being paid to Philip Lord Wharton and Sir Thomas, his son, acquitting the tenants of all further liabilities and "in consideration of the Honourable care, respect and affection which the said Philip Lord Wharton and Sir Thomas Wharton have and beare to the aforesaid Tenants parties to these presents" etc.

It was also confirmed that the tenants had the right to cut hedgerow trees for their use, but timber growing in woods could be taken only with the consent of the lord's steward and only if needed for necessary repairs to buildings or for husbandry. The Whartons in their turn reserved to themselves and their heirs the mining rights and the taking of any timber necessary for the carrying out of such works. And finally the tenants agreed to continue to "make ffealty and suite of Court to the said Philip Lord Wharton" etc. ... "at the Court Leet or Court Baron to be holden at Muacre aforesaid, and pay their Greenhewes[5] and ffishings and all other dueties as at all tymes theretofore they have usually and accustombably done" etc ..

This system of land tenure was carried on generation after generation under the Wharton family and their successors, until the "copyhold" estate was abolished by legislation in 1925. The land-lords were then given compensation for the loss of their customary fines and rents. This was payable by the tenants over a period of up to 15 years, when their lands were declared freehold for ever.

Towards the end of this "copyhold" period, manor courts were held either at the "Queens Head" or the "Kings Head" inns at Muker[6], but when these public houses gave up their licences, the annual court repaired to the "Farmers Arms". The court consisted of 12 jurymen together with the lord of the manor's steward, his agent, and the bailiff. One of the latter's duties was to act as town crier and the following is the wording of the proclamation made in 1905 by William Thos. Raw, bailiff, before the business of the court commenced:-

Proclamation of the Manor Court for Muker
W.T. Raw, Bailiff 1905

Proclamation out of doors   "Oyez — Oyez — Oyez"

"All persons who have any business to transact at the Court
Baron, and customary Court, of Francis Horner Lyell etc.
Lord of the Manor of Muker, are requested to attend the same
now being holden"

"God Save the King"

Proclamation in Court   "Oyez — Oyez — Oyez"

"All persons who owe Suit and Service at the Court Baron, and
Copyhold and Customary Court of Francis Horner Lyell Esq.
etc. Draw near and give your attendance, and answer your names
when called, otherwise you will be amerced".[7]

"God Save the King"

Proclamation for Heirs   "Oyez — Oyez — Oyez"

"Heirs of ..... come into Court and take your admittance of the
Property of which they ..... died. Seized otherwise the same will
become forfeited to the Lord of the Manor."

"None appearing seizing was awarded".

(1) "bovate or oxgang" — 15 acres or as much land as an ox can plough in one
season.
(2) "toft" — a house or cottage.
(3) "cumin" — aromatic seeds of a plant of the parsley family; said to be a cure
for flatulence.
(4) largely against the Scots.
(5) greenhewes — probably a charge made by the lord of the manor enabling
tenants to gather green branches, shrubs, wild fruit and nuts from the forest
for their own use and for cattle feed.
(6) Manor courts were also held at the "Buck Inn", Reeth, although the whole of
Arkengarthdale and parts of Grinton parish had already become freehold.
(7) fined.

Philip, the Fourth Lord Wharton

OF ALL THE LORDS of the Swaledale Manors, Philip, 4th Lord Wharton, was probably the most distinguished. Although he was an absentee landlord like those who came after him, he took a great interest in his Swaledale estates. He developed the lead-mining industry, looking after the welfare of the miners, especially their moral welfare. He helped those who suffered persecution for their religious beliefs.

He came from a family whose members varied in character and stability, but they were nearly all able and ambitious, and wealthy in land and possessions. Many Whartons sought favour with the reigning Monarchs of their time and succeeded in obtaining political and military preferments for which they received generous payments. Almost all made judicious marriages adding further to the estates which descended to their children. Some, however, were influenced by the extravagances of the period in which they lived, and dissipated the wealth which had been handed down to them. On the other hand at least two Whartons, (Philip the 4th Lord being one) were noted for their religious beliefs and upheld the Puritanism and Nonconformity of the time.

The first Wharton to be mentioned was one Gilbert de Querton, as it was spelt, who, in 1292, successfully proved, before the justices at Appleby, his right to the Manor of Querton (otherwise Wharton Hall near Kirkby Stephen). From him was descended Sir Thos. Wharton (1495-1568) who was created Baron Wharton by King Henry VIII for his military services against the Scots. In addition, in 1544, he was granted what later became the manor of Muker. This was part of the Rievaulx Abbey estates confiscated by the Crown at the time of the Dissolution of the monasteries. He later received half the Manor of Healaugh (Swaledale) from Philip and Mary. These manors eventually descended to his great-great-grandson, Philip, with whom we are now specially concerned.

Philip was the elder son of Sir Thos. Wharton (1587-1622) of Aske Hall, near Richmond, and Philadelphia, his wife. He was born in 1613 and succeeded his grandfather in 1625 at the age of 12 as the fourth baron. He inherited an income of £8,000, with estates in Westmorland, Aske, and Healaugh Park, in the Ainsty of York. In his youth he was "one of the handsomest men and the greatest beau of his times; he had particularly fine legs, and took great delight to show them in dancing". Nevertheless he developed a serious frame of mind and became a strong Puritan in his religious beliefs. He was a friend of Oliver Cromwell, and took a minor role in the Civil War but declined to take an active part in the government of the Republic. He disapproved of the execution of King Charles I and refused to sit in the House of Lords, after which his relations with Cromwell became strained.

He married, firstly Elizabeth, daughter and heir of Sir Rowland Wandesford. She died soon afterwards, however, and Philip re-married in 1637 Jane, daughter and heir of Arthur Goodwin, M.P., a colonel in the Parliamentary Army. The latter died in 1643 leaving her the manors of Winchendon, near Aylesbury, and Wooburn, near Cookham. She and Philip lived at Winchendon until she died in 1658, after which he removed to Wooburn, an old palace[1] formerly belonging to the Bishops of Lincoln. Philip married thirdly Anne, daughter of William Carr. These three wives gave him a number of children and Jane left him those two very nice properties in Buckinghamshire.

Now to his connection with Swaledale. In 1645, he served on a committee for removing "scandalous" (i.e. inefficient, immoral or Royalist) parsons from their livings. In a letter to Lord Fairfax in that year he expressed a wish that upon the sequestration of Grinton vicarage, "an honest, faithful, godly man might be put in, who might be of bold spirit and an able body". "Most of the dale", he added, "are in my hands, and I would be exceeding glad, therefore, out of that respect, as well as the general, that it were well supplied."

Living mostly in the South, Philip took care that his Yorkshire estates were administered by capable stewards and agents. It was customary at that time for moble families to employ as servants members of families of a lesser order but of good breeding. He therefore appointed a Quaker attorney, Philip Swale of Richmond, to take care of his Swaledale properties and to help develop the lead-mines. Swale was the son of Robert and Mary Swale who were servants in the household of Philadelphia, the 4th Lord's mother, who continued to live at Aske Hall during her widowhood. Robt. Swale was a relation of Solomon Swale of Swale Hall, Grinton.

In 1622 Philadelphia had made this undertaking:

"Know that I, Philadelphia, lady Wharton, Wydow, have and doe promise to give unto Robert Swale my Servant the some of Twentie poundes in money the same to be paid upon the day

that the said Robert Swale shall enter marrie with my servant
Mary Etherington which shall be in lieu of a gift which I doe
promise to bestowe upon him with the said Mary Etherington
in witness whereof I have here unto sett my hand the XXth
day of february Anno. Dm. 1622"

         £20   Phill. Wharton"

Aske Hall became occupied in 1651 by Sir Thomas Wharton
(1615-1684) and in that year he leased to Robert Swale, Mary Swale
and Philip Swale, the manor house at Hartforth near Richmond. It is
understandable that Philip Swale, growing up in close association with
the Wharton family should have been chosen by the 4th Lord to
administer his Swaledale estates.

In spite of his Puritan activities Wharton was included in the
King's amnesty at the Restoration of Charles II in 1660. With the
passing of the Act of Uniformity in 1662, two thousand dissenting
parsons were deprived of their livings for refusing to submit to the
ritual of the Anglican church, the episcopal ordination, and the acceptance of the book of Common Prayer. Lord Wharton helped many of
them with money and friendship. One of these was John Gunter, his
steward at Healaugh Park, near York. In 1677 Wharton was imprisoned
in the Tower of London for 5 months for questioning the legality
of Parliament's adjournment for 15 months. Following the accession
of James II in 1685 he and Anne, his third wife, thought it wise to
spend a year travelling in France and Germany.

Upon his return he found that his relationship with his
Swaledale tenants was deteriorating. Like most landlords of the
period, he had been endeavouring to obtain increased or "inhanced"
rents. Costs were rising and his various family commitments were
considerable. In 1685 Wharton brought a Common Pleas Suit against
Edward Milner, John Wharton, Anthony Milner, Thomas Calvert,
James Coates, Ralph Kearton, Alexander Raw, William Kearton, William
Arundel, Henry Clarkson, James Fryer and Thomas Raw, all yeomen
of Grinton parish. (It is interesting to note that nearly all these surnames exist in the dale today). Wharton maintained that the above
tenants had broken an agreement for the payment of certain
"gressoms"[2] and inhanced rents. The plaintiffs denied that
promises were ever made and finally the case went against Lord
Wharton. The tenants were awarded 100s damages which they later
freely refunded to his lordship.

On Aug 20th, 1685, John Gunter wrote from Healaugh Park to
Philip Swale as follows: "I have not heard from his Lordship since the
28th July. I have writt twice or thrice since, at which I am not a
little troubled, the rather because I left him much impaired in his
health, and his legg broaken out in the old soar, for the reason

whereof some Phisitians advised him going into Fraunce to try the ayre this summer season for a month or two."

He had indeed gone to France but before he left he gave Philip Swale very detailed instructions regarding additions and restorations to Aske Hall, including the laying of "a fair slope for Coaches and Horses to go up from the meadow to the lower part of the said court, and another fair slope from the lower part of the said court to the upper part ....."

With regard to the lead mines Wharton had brought into the dale two or three experts from the mines in Derbyshire. John Renshaw and Adam Barker were two of these, and they eventually became, along with Philip Swale, working partners with his lordship in exploiting the Swaledale lead.

When Philip Swale died in 1687, Lord Wharton wrote the following to the former's executor, John Chaytor:-

"I received yours of the 7th of Oct. which gave me notice of the Death of my Old and usefull Servant, with a copy of his will inclosed I would not inlarge unnecessarily. In truth the newes of his death doth much affect me and I doubt will much disorder the various affaires I had under his charge. I add no more upon this Subject but desire to submitt to the will of the Alwise disposing God.

I perceive by his will that he hath given you & the rest of his Exors. his interest in my leadworkes in Swaledale (amongst others). It is most certaine that no partners ever had a more friendly correspondence than was amongst us & therefore it will (even upon common fame) concern you who are to come in his place that there may be the like continued.

I need not but must minde you that all the books of accounts be kept & as near as can be the same method be used in keeping of the books as formerly in his time.

As to what may belong to the management of the ffeildes upon the place I suppose it will be found fitt to leave it in the hands of James ffryer & Adam Barker that they proceed & have all the powers they had. And that Joseph Etherington[3] may keepe the books and enter all accounts as he did in his Masters time ....."

After James II had given up the crown and fled the country, Lord Wharton was one of the first to welcome William and Mary. He received William at Wooburn in 1689; and Queen Mary, in 1690, "came from Windsor and dined unexpectedly with Lady Wharton, who was hard put to it to find food, having only a little maid as cook". The first consequence of the new reign was the passing of the Act of Toleration which at last gave Dissenters lawful permission to worship in their own chapels or meeting-houses. Lord Wharton built a meeting-house adjoining his shooting lodge of Smarber Hall, above Low Row, which was registered at the Thirsk Quarter Sessions in 1691. It was intended for the benefit of the lead-miners in that part of Swaledale.

The fourth Lord Wharton is remembered for his Bible Charity. In 1692, he conveyed some of his land near Healaugh (York) to Nonconformist trustees, the proceeds of which were to be used for the buying and distributing each year of 1,050 Bibles and catechisms to children who had learnt by heart seven specified psalms and were living in certain towns and villages on his estates in Yorkshire, Westmorland, Cumberland and Buckinghamshire. The trust also directed that 10s should be given to a minister to preach one sermon annually. During the beginning of the last century, owing to negligence in replacing Nonconformist trustees who had died, it fell into the hands of the Church of England. Their clergy then distributed the Bibles along with the church catechism and the book of Common Prayer, except in Swaledale where a vigorous opposition was able to keep the distribution in accordance with the original terms made by the founder. Eventually an agreement was reached in 1898 between the Congregational Church and the Church of England stipulating that the Bibles be distributed without distinction to scholars in Sunday Schools both Anglican and Nonconformist. There is hardly a Swaledale family which does not possess one of these "Wharton Bibles".

The fourth Lord died at Hampstead in 1696 and upon his elaborate mural monument in Wooburn church there is an inscription in Latin which, translated, states that he was:- "an active supporter of the English constitution, a loyal observer, advocate, and patron of the reformed religion, a model alike of good works and of a true and living faith." He had three wives and was the father of fifteen children of whom nine reached maturity.

---

(1) Philip, the 4th Lord, is said to have spent £100,000 on improvements to the old palace. It later came into possession of three successive owners, the last of whom, a member of the Bertie family, had it pulled down in 1750. Its contents were sold for £800.

(2) a fine paid by a tenant upon the death of a landlord, or upon an alienation of a tenancy.

(3) Joseph was probably related to Philip Swale, whose mother was Mary Etherington.

Quarter Session Records of the Seventeenth Century

THE CONFISCATION OF the monastic houses and lands by Henry VIII, and the conversion of their resources for the benefit of the Exchequer, brought big changes into the dale. The Abbots of Rievaulx and the Priors of Bridlington no longer controlled the destinies of many Swaledale folk. The "church of St. Andrew .... with Grinton and all its vicinity" together with Muker and Upper Swaledale now became Crown property, but not for long. The area comprising what is now the Manor of Muker was granted to Thomas, the first Lord Wharton as mentioned previously. He later bought from the Crown part of the Manor of Healaugh and, for 200 years, the Wharton family held sway. West Grinton, Harkerside and Whitaside, formerly held by Bridlington Priory, was sold in 1599 to Richard Wiseman, a goldsmith, and Francis Fitch, both of London.

All these new landlords tended to interfere with the customs and rights which the tenants had enjoyed under the religious houses. For nearly a hundred years thereafter were records of law-suits in which the inhabitants successfully resisted encroachments upon their privileges. It is said that the Englishmen of that time had a passion for litigation, and when one examines the history of the period one feels that the dalesmen were not behind hand in guarding their rights by recourse to law. Petty disputes over boundaries, waterways and trespass were usually settled by the manor courts, at which the lord of the manor or his steward sat in the seat of justice, with the tenants around to see fair play.

The more serious offences, i.e. those committed against the laws of the realm, were dealt with by local justices of the peace. Exceptional cases such as treason or murder were sent to the King's judges sitting at the assizes at York Castle. There was a saying that "the law ended at Reeth". Indeed it would appear that the law stopped some distance below Reeth. The inhabitants certainly revolted against the multitude of petty regulations which Parliament thought were necessary to keep the peace. The records of the North Riding Quarter Sessions reveal many of the problems which confronted our ancestors.

From the beginning of the reign of Queen Elizabeth I, the administration of the law was in the hands of the local justices of the peace. Quarter Sessions were held at Richmond and other North Riding towns. The duties of the Justices were varied and comprehensive. They controlled the daily affairs of village life, corrected unruly servants, removed from the district idle and incorrigible beggars, and punished lewd and bawdy persons, tale-tellers and slanderers, and those engaged in unlawful sports. They imposed fines upon those who failed to attend church and, later on, licensed the meeting-places of Nonconformists. They relieved the poor and needy, licensed alehouses and fixed the price of liquor and, above all, saw that the inhabitants maintained the roads and bridges which, in Swaledale, were essential to its prosperity.

In 1604, we read of John Maye of Grinton, being fined with others "for keeping unlicenced alehouses". Ten years later Margery Atkinson appeared at court for selling ale at tenpence a gallon. At the Richmond Quarter Sessions in 1606 the following was recorded:-

"Whereas Henry Simpson of Grinton, Clerk, having made oath that he is in fear of his life or burning his house by Henry Simpson (sic) of Reeth, John Dowglasse and Matthew Blaides of Grinton, a warrant be made to attach to the said three persons and bring them before the next Justice ... at the next sessions."

At the Richmond sessions in 1613, John Blaides of Grinton, Geoffrey Garth of Reeth, Yeoman, Bigot Blades and Edward Blades of Hull, cordwainers, were fined ...

" ... for riotous assembly and assault on the wife and servant of one Geo. Alderson of Cogden, gent, breaking the Windows etc." At Thirsk ...

" ... a Grinton man (no name given) to stand upon the pillory at Richmond on Saturday next in open market for the space of an hour being convicted for stealing Sir Marmaduke Wyvill's deer,"

and in 1615

" ... two Grinton men for playing cards".

An echo of the civil war persisted in 1653, when the parish officers of Grinton were ordered to provide for a woman of Fremington and her three small children, her husband having been killed in the service of the Parliamentary forces and "in case any fail, a gentleman to see right done". At Richmond in 1652, a yeoman of Healey (Healaugh) was fined fifteen shillings for playing at bowls, and other unlawful games and selling tobacco upon the Lord's Day (the fine went to the poor of the parish); and in 1654, a Reeth yeoman for selling oatmeal, peas and tobacco on a Sunday. Unlike the Vicar of Bray, some dalesmen stuck to their republican sympathies despite the fact that the Monarchy had become restored in the person of Charles II in 1660. A year after this date, a presentment was made of —

" ... a yeoman of Keld in the parish of Grinton for uttering these seditious and defamatory words to another yeoman. 'Thou had best be quiet, for those that thou buildest upon, I hope they will not last long, and that I lived as well when there was no King and I hope to do so again, when there will be no King'."

... and two years later James Arundel, yeoman, appeared before the Justices for —

" ... having said to Simon Douglas of Fremington 'Thou and thy father are rogues and traitors, and all are traitors that doth fight for the King'."

Cromwell died on 3rd September, 1657 and taking the opposite view, in 1658 Robert Myles of Marrick was called to the Richmond Quarter Sessions for encouraging sedition, discord and rebellion and using such scandalous words as —

" ... that Oliver, Lord Protector, was burning in hell fire, for taking so many honest gentlemen's lives away."

However the bill against him was ignored.

The plague of London was raging in 1665 and spread to other parts of England. Fearing its consequences in the North Riding, rogues and vagabonds were refused entry to villages and the inhabitants were warned to keep a look out and prevent suspected carriers of the plague from staying in their homes. On the 8th August, 1665, the Richmond Quarter Sessions ordered that —

" ... six men of Marske do diligently from time to time, day and night at namely, two of the night and one of the day, for 40 days next coming ..."

... watch the house of George Mason and ensure that he or his family do not leave and mingle with other people in Marske, as he had just returned from London and might be carrying the plague.

In 1609 all the inhabitants of Grinton were charged for not repairing the highway between Whitaside and Richmond. Regarding bridges, certain of the more important ones were classified as County bridges and their upkeep was the responsibility of all the wapentakes of the North Riding. The cost of building and repairing was assessed to each district, according to its means. Grinton Bridge was re-built about 1575, costing two hundred pounds. Ten years earlier an assessment was made for "re-edifying, repayringe and amendment" of Grinton Bridge which was probably built of wood at that time.

At the Richmond Quarter Sessions of July 1613 John Hutchinson and Charles Hutchinson of Reeth got into trouble. They diverted Arkle beck at Ellers from its proper course, using large stones which they took from Sir Timothy Hutton's West Close. What their object was is not stated, but the effect was rather serious, inasmuch as the diverted stream did one hundred marks[1] damage to New Close, Tenth Close and West Close, and, more serious still, played havoc with Grinton bridge and the road there.

Exactly a year later, it was reported that Grinton bridge had fallen in decay. Whether this was the result of the Hutchinsons' action twelve months earlier, one can only surmise. However, Sir Timothy Hutton repaired the damage at his own initiative, the cost being thirteen pounds.

[1] one mark = 13s. 4d.

The Lead Miners

THE HILLSIDES and moors of Swaledale are pitted and scarred by old lead workings, evidence of an industry which in its most prosperous days employed four thousand men in Swaledale and Arkengarthdale. As mentioned earlier, the Romans were probably the first to exploit the rich veins on the moors above Fremington Edge and at Hurst.

There are no records to show that the Saxon and Scandinavian settlers mined for lead, but Crown papers of Henry II state that the mines in the Honour of Richmond, which included the Hurst and Old Gang mines, were affiliated to mines on Alston Moor. In 1182 AD lead ingots were being carried in pony trains from Arkengarthdale to Yarm-on-Tees for export. The Abbot of Jervaulx in Wensleydale bought lead for roofing the abbey. Between 1307 and 1327, lead was one of the commodities offered for sale at Richmond market, and, along with other produce, was taxed as a means of raising money for the building of the town wall; "for every cartload of lead — two pence".

The Guildhall records of 1560-1 at York give dock charges of fourteen pounds, fourteen shillings and twopence, paid into the city funds for the unloading of lead at the Old Crane, Skeldergate. This may have reached the city, which was a port at that time, by barge from Boroughbridge. In 1684 from Yarm and Stockton went consignments of lead to Peter le Clarke, a factor at Bruges, to Ralph Harrison at Rotterdam, and to other places on the continent. Leland, the sixteenth century antiquary and traveller, in his "Itinerary of England" wrote —

> "Grinton is a little Market Towne ... the Market is of Corne and Linyn Cloth for Men of Suadale, the which be much usid in digging Lead Oure. On eche side of Suadale be greate Hilles where they digge. Little corne groweth in Suadale."

Up to the end of the seventeenth century lead was extracted from surface pits or "bell pits" as they were called. Traces of these can be found on most of the mining fields. Vertical shafts were sunk until a vein was exposed and the men, with pick and hammer, broke up the lead ore which was brought to the surface in baskets by hand-winches, or carried up ladders. The pits were often dug in rows along the veins and connected by lateral passages. When the veins were exhausted, or when the shafts became water-logged, the workings were abandoned and trials made elsewhere. Sometimes the miners struck old workings which were always referred to as "t'owd man".

Philip, the Fourth Lord Wharton, lord of the Healaugh Manor, with others in partnership, owned the Friarfold mines. John Renshaw, his manager, reporting upon the operations in 1685, said that Adam Barker (the joint manager) had opened a new shaft of seventeen fathoms deep at Lownathwaite —

" ... but how farr the oulde man hath gone they could not tell, neither was they come to the vaine, but hopes in time, though uncertain when, to see how the oulde man hath left that worke ...[1]

"Att Merifielde they have sunke a new shafte, att 14 fathom, they come to a greate feedar of water, they [made] a sumpe 8 fathom to meet that shafte, betwixt wich they were forced to boare 13 fathom to take off that water, which boare-hole was 2 inch and a halfe and near filled with watter ... but in sinking that 13 fathom, after it was boared, the boarhole stoped 3 times ... which they had much difficulty to open, & the last time it stoped it rise soe fast that the workmen fled and left it, but A.B.[2] immediatelye went down & after the water had risen above a mans height, leapt into it in his clothes as he was, & dived 3 times to the bottome of the watter, & by providence removed whatt stoped the watter, otherwys that worke [would] have been lost, an action [which] whoulde have dread most men to have done, besides the prejudish to health, but I thanke god he received noe harme, but the wetteing of his clothes, which I hope none will be against giving him recompenses for it ..."

Another old method of getting lead-ore was by means of "hushing". A promising slope was selected, where ore was known to exist. Above this was constructed a dam or reservoir, the sides of which were made of turf and stones. When a large store of water had been gathered, the dam was broken, allowing the water to rush down the hillside. In its course it tore away the subsoil, removing stones, clay and gravel, and, if the site had been well-chosen, laid bare the veins of lead-ore. It was then a comparatively easy matter for the miners to work with pick and shovel, uncovering more of the veins which the water had partially exposed. There are many of these old "hushes" to be found. This method went on until quite recent times and some of the old "hush" gullies became deep clefts in the hillsides.[3]

There is evidence that the Cistercian Abbots of Rievaulx, who had been granted what is now the Muker Manor, in 1241-2, were interested in lead-mining. In the Chartulary of Rievaulx Abbey are mentioned the names of Radulph, John and Nicholas Alderson, who, in the time of Henry VIII, were bailiffs, being responsible for the upkeep and supervision of their woods and leadmines in Swaledale. Bridlington Priory, which had received a grant of the manor of Grinton in 1120, likewise took an interest in the lead-mines.

As mentioned earlier, the Healaugh Manor which included Reeth and what is now the Manor of Muker, came into the possession of the Wharton family after the dissolution of the monasteries in 1538-9. They and their successors lived outside the dale, but derived a considerable income from the rich deposits of lead. They not only leased small areas to local men, but engaged in mining themselves, employing agents and business managers. After the Duke of Wharton died in 1731 part of his Healaugh Manor passed into the hands of Lord Pomfret. His practice was to appoint outsiders to manage his mines. He apparently could not trust the dalesmen, who were apt to be biased in favour of the workmen: quite naturally, for they were of the same stock and blood and the dalesmen were noted for their clannishness. Writing in 1773 he said —

"... to have just account and to make a full profit of the Estates of the Mines in Swaledale is *not* to employ anyone as Steward who is a Yorkshireman, and particularly of that neighbourhood."

As a matter of fact, since records began, one comes across the names of "foreigners" to the dales, acting in the capacity of "steward" or "manager" to the lord. Adam Barker and John Renshaw, mentioned earlier, were both Derbyshire men and had had experience of the lead-mines in that county before they were appointed by Philip, Fourth Lord Wharton to look after his lordship's interests.[4] Miners and agents came from mining areas further afield still. Thomas Rosewarne, Agent at the How lead-mines, who died in 1765, came from Cornwall. One comes across other Cornish names in the Grinton Parish registers such as Benanack, Benullock, Hawkins and Trigeare. In prosperous times the dale also attracted miners from Westmorland and Cumberland, with such names as Nicholson, Brunskill, Fothergill, Wharton, Harrison, Laidman, Bousfield, Waller and Morland.

One curious name which appears in the Grinton and Arkengarthdale Parish registers from the seventeenth century onwards, is that of COLSISON. The first is that of Peter Colsison who died in 1666. In the account given by W.G. Collingwood of the German miners who settled at Keswick in 1564 to 1577 to work the copper-mines under a Charter from Queen Elizabeth, mention is made of a Peter

KOLSSEISON, a copper-smith by trade. He came all the way from Southern Bavaria and married Elizabeth Walker of Dalehead, near Keswick. He had numerous descendants, one of whom, another Peter, lived at Fremington, where he applied his expert knowledge of ore-smelting. His German name had already been crystallised to COLSISON and given an English spelling, but nevertheless it is spelt in eighteen different ways in the Grinton Parish registers.

The eighteenth and nineteenth centuries saw big changes in lead-mining practice. The veins were worked at lower altitudes and, instead of shafts, levels or adits were driven horizontally into the hillsides. The chief advantage of this was that it got rid of water which ran out at the entrance to the levels. Water-wheels, pumping machinery and later, steam engines, were introduced, which facilitated the excavation and treatment of the ore. But these things needed capital and companies were formed to take over the richer areas. The local gentry, as well as outsiders, invested their money in these ventures and fortunes were made. The days of the independent mine operators who leased small areas of moorland were over. They could not compete with the capitalized organisations and were squeezed out. Such famous names as The Old Gang Company, The A.D. Company, The London Lead Company and the South Swaledale Lead Mining Company employed the available male population, and such was the demand for labour, that it brought into the dale a further influx of strangers. A resident of Reeth living at the turn of the eighteenth century wrote that, previously, the dale was occupied by a peculiarly primitive people and that few men from the outside world made their appearance among them. But with the coming of these "foreigners" customs began to change and many dialect words which were expressive and comprehensive became obsolete.

The census returns of the early nineteenth century revealed that more men were employed in the mines than worked in agriculture. Some miners tried to acquire small-holdings where they could keep cows and sheep. A few succeeded, against pressure from the old farming population. It was an advantage to have a stake in food production, especially as mining wages were invariably low and unemployment frequent, when weather conditions left some of the mines unworkable during long periods. Working in the open air was also a healthy change from the damp, and often poisonous atmosphere of the pits and shafts.

Mining brought with it many accidents, often fatal. William March, who died in 1803 and was parish clerk at Grinton for fifty-two years, mentioned incidences of these in the registers of burials. No less than fourteen of the parish were killed in the twenty-five years between 1755 and 1780. Many also were incapacitated through

Philip, 4th Lord Wharton, aged about 19. Portrait by Sir Anthony van Dyck (courtesy of the National Gallery of Art, Washington, D.C., Andrew Mellon Collection).

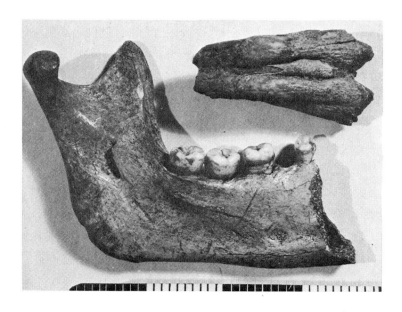

Part of jaw of Bronze Age man discovered by a gamekeeper at West Arngill, and tooth of wild ox found nearby.

Reeth about 1900, with the 'Half Moon Inn' on the right.

Local institutions. Above: The last of the Manor Courts at Muker on June 4th, 1924. Below: The Reeth Union Board of Guardians, about 1910.

Swaledale hostelries. Above: The old 'Kings' Head' at Muker, which was demolished and replaced by Brentwood Lodge. Below: A view taken about 1870 of a draper's shop at Reeth which now forms the dining room of the 'Black Bull.'

accident. Some succumbed to consumption, the dreaded "miners' disease", brought about by breathing dust and foul air.

Living accommodation for the newcomers to mining was appalling. Some lived near the site of their work, but others were taken as boarders in the villages and hamlets. Mortality, as will be shewn in a later chapter, became exceptionally high.

(1) As this reference was made in 1685, "the oulde man" in this case was probably mining the lead-ore in the Middle Ages or even before.

(2) Adam Barker.

(3) i.e. Lover Gill Hush and Providence Hush under Muker Common, Bunting Hush (Gunnerside Gill), Beldi Hill Hush near Keld, Hungry Hushes opposite the C.B. Inn (Arkengarthdale), and many others.

(4) Adam Barker and his family stayed in Swaledale and some of his descendants live there to this day.

Arthur Young's Visit in 1770

ARTHUR YOUNG was an eminent agricultural authority living in the late eighteenth century. He was at one time the Secretary of the Board of Agriculture, and one of his duties was to make himself familiar with agricultural practices in every part of the country. The following extracts are taken from "A Six Months Tour Through the North of England", "an account of the present state of Agriculture (letter ix) published in 1770". In it he describes what he saw whilst travelling on horseback down Arkengarthdale to Askrigg.

"From Brough, the road, if I may give it that name, to Askrig, lies over one continued range of mountains, here called moors. The cultivated valleys are too inconsiderable to deserve a mention. Most of these fifteen miles, however dreadful the road, are tracts of very improveable land; if a good turnpike road was made from Askrig to Brough, the first great step to cultivation would be over; for it is almost impossible to improve a country with spirit, the roads of which are impassable. It is extremely melancholy to view such tracts of land that are indisputably capable of yielding many beneficial crops, lie totally waste; etc. ..."

"From Askrig to Reeth and Fremington the country is mountainous, and full of lead-mines."

Here he adds a note:

"In which many hundreds of people are employed, the men can earn at an average 1s.3d a day; the women 1s and boys and girls from 4d to 9d. But the day's work finishes by twelve, or one o'clock, after which no bribes are sufficient to tempt them into the farmer's service in the busiest times, even for an hour."

He then continues his description:

" ... the vales are all grass enclosures, rich and let very high.

"The soil is in general a rich loam and a red gravel, lets from 20s to 40s an acre: these grass farmers occupy from £5 to £60 a year. As to the management, it is, as you may suppose, not very complex. Their manuring consists chiefly in using peat and coal ashes; the last of which they reckon best on wettish lands.

"Their stock is chiefly cows, and horses to carry lead; an acre will in some years keep a cow, but not often; and in some it requires three or four acres. Their breed of cattle is the short horns: and the size of their swine up to 20 stone.

"The summer's milk of a cow is worth £5.10s; the common quantity four gallons a day. It is all fold; no dairies.

"In winter the cows' feed is hay alone, of which they eat 1½ acre per head. They suckle their calves a week for killing; but not at all for rearing. The summer joist[1] is 35s.

"Their flocks of sheep rise as high as 500, by means of turning on the moors. The profit they reckon at 10s. a head; they keep them all winter and spring on the moors, but give them hay in deep snows. The average fleece of wool, 3½ lb. Land sells at 30 years purchase. Tythes generally gathered.

"Poor rates 1s. 3d in the pound. They are all employed either in the lead mines or in knitting. All drink tea."[2]

Arthur Young then gives the prices of commodities and brief particulars of some of the farms

Mutton	3d	(a lb)
Veal	3½d	(a lb)
Pork	3d	(a lb)
Milk	1½ pint at 1d	
Potatoes	6d	a peck
Turnips	2d	a peck
Candles	6d	(a lb)
Soap	6d	(a lb)
House rent	25s	(a year)
Firing	35s	(a year)

	"Building	
Mason	per day	1s 6d
Carpenter		1s 6d
Thatcher		1s 6d

Farmhouses of stone and slate

"the general economy of these little farmers will appear from the following sketches:-

"One of them has

55 acres all grass	3 young cattle
£52 rent	200 sheep
7 cows	1 boy
1 fatting beast	1 maid

"Another

40 acres of grass	100 sheep
£49 rent	1 man
6 cows	
2 young cattle	

"Another

20 acres of grass	3 cows
£35 rent	200 sheep

"Another

55 acres	300 sheep
£60 rent	1 boy
8 cows	1 maid"

---

(1) a joist = agistment, the profit made from letting a pasture for grazing of another person's cattle.

(2) Tea became a popular beverage after about 1750. Arthur Young considered this a pernicious habit. In "Farming Letter" he wrote that "as much superfluous money is expended on tea and sugar as would maintain four million more subjects on bread."

Commons and Enclosures

A VISITOR making his first acquaintance with Swaledale is invariably struck by the multiplicity of field walls, some of which enclose very small areas. When the first Norse settlers had built their rough rectangular houses of stone and turf, they cleared the ground adjoining and made small "garths" or "closes", into which they brought their animals for the night, or during inclement weather.

In the summer months the pigs, sheep, goats and kine were allowed to browse together on the rough hill-sides. When an increasing number of people settled in the dale and turned their animals out to feed, it became necessary to regularise the grazing so that the common land should not become exhausted. Village committees, known as "bye-law men", were elected to enforce rules whereby each owner of a house or tenement was permitted to graze or "stint" on the common land a certain number of animals, the total of which was no more than the land could bear. Fines were inflicted upon those who exceeded their permitted "stint". The number of beasts each farmer could loose on to the common pastures was based originally upon the money value of his house or tenement and existing enclosed fields. This was expressed in so many "gaits". An old 19th century agreement regularized the grazing on Muker pastures as follows:- four gaits would allow four geld or barren ewes; or three ewe sheep and their followers; or three tups; or one cow of any age; or one yearling stagg (young horse); or one mule; or eight geese. Eight "gaits" would permit one horse above two years, and nine "gaits" one mare and foal, and so on.

During the 18th or 19th centuries this old system of land tenure began to change. The larger farmers and landowners saw that, by enclosing the common land and attaching the enclosures to their existing holdings, they increased the value of their estates. Previous to this time, slices of common land were enclosed by agreement and sometimes by forceful means. Endless disputes over boundaries ensued, so that the Government passed laws whereby common land could be enclosed only by a special Act of Parliament.

The first piece of common land in Swaledale to be divided in this manner was Fremington Edge and moor in 1778. Thomas Elliott, the owner of Fremington Hall at that time, was probably the driving spirit behind this. He certainly stood to gain the biggest share of this division. Arthur Young wrote that "Elliott was one of the greatest improvers of moors in Yorkshire." The latter had estates in Craven (Arncliffe) as well as in Swaledale and laid it down as a maxim never to attempt any improvement without enclosing. He takes a field every year; but the first work is surrounding it with a stone wall.

The Fremington Enclosure Act, copies of which still exist in printed form[1], sets out the methods by which this enclosure was to be accomplished. It is headed as follows: "An Act for Dividing and Inclosing Fremington Edge and Fremington Moor and certain Waste Grounds in the Township of Fremington, in the Parish of Grinton in the North Riding of the County of York." The names of the chief supplicants were Thomas Elliott, Thomas Hutchinson, Richard Metcalfe, Richard Robinson, Henry Alderson, Ralph Brockill, William March and Thomas Stodart, and several small farmers, representing 28 ownerships in all. The area involved was only 1075 acres of which Thos. Elliott secured over one-third.

The Act implied that it would be to the advantage of the several owners if the moors were divided and enclosed, their shares being allotted to them in proportion to the value of their existing holdings. William Brown of Thoralby, George Jackson of Richmond and Thomas Humphrey of Scorton were appointed to act as commissioners and to "swear by oath to divide etc. — without Favour or Affection, Prejudice or Malice." It was arranged that George Jackson and William Fothergill of Carr End, Wensleydale, should survey the area and make a plan.

At least three meetings to allow for objections were held before the act could be carried into force. Notices of the times of these meetings were fixed upon "the Great Door of the Parish Church of Grinton". The commissioners got busy. First of all the boundaries were ridden or perambulated. Public or private ways and roads were set out, also common quarries, wells, water-courses and watering-places for the use of the proprietors and made accessible from their future allotments. Accommodation roads were planned, the herbage of which was to be used by those who farmed the adjoining allotments. Having defined the access roads, the remaining ground was pegged out and allotted to the various owners, always taking into consideration the quality and situation of the division. Any doubts as to the fairness of the allocations were brought before the commissioners, who were required to look into all claims and examine all witnesses on oath, or "being of the People called Quakers, by solemn affirmation".[2] Upon the evidence submitted, the commissioners judged as they thought right.

Within six months after the execution of the award, the partici-
pators were each required to give his assent or acceptance at a
public meeting, notice of which was given out after Divine service
upon some suitable Sunday. Owners of the new allotments were
obliged to fence and enclose them at their own expense. If they
defaulted, complaints could be made to a Justice of the Peace, who
would then direct the fences to be erected, the cost of which was
charged to the parties defaulting.

When the allocation was completed, an Award was enrolled and
entered at the Registry Office at Northallerton and a copy made
available to each person interested, at 2d a sheet. The original
document was then lodged "in a good Oak Box ... provided for that
Purpose, with a lock ... and key" and placed in the vestry of Grinton
Church, the Vicar to hold the key. For their pains, the commissioners
received one guinea a day for every day's attendance on the job and
7/6d for expenses attending each meeting. The surveyors got 6d for
every acre of ground measured, planned and staked out, plus 5/- per
day each, whilst in attendance upon the commissioners. All these
costs, together with the expenses of promoting the Bill to be passed
by Parliament, were divided proportionally between those participating.

The Act confirmed that the King would continue to retain any
mineral rights upon the land enclosed, would retain the right of
working any existing or future mines, and would have access over
the land for this purpose. He could also authorize the building of
smelt-mills and other works in connection therewith. Neither were
the rights of the tithe owners prejudiced, nor of the persons who had
existing way-leaves to and over the moors. The Award was dated 11th
Mar. 1778 and the result was approximately to treble the areas of
each holding. The new allotments had to be walled with stone within
12 months, according to the following specification:-

"seven Quarters High[3] exclusive of Coap and Coble[4] ...
2 rows of Throughs[5] at proper distances ... 30" wide at the
bottom and tapering gradually to 16" wide at the top."

Some of the 28 owners who were entitled to share in the
division were obviously small cottagers. Whether they were all able
to afford their proportions of the cost of wall-making and the
expenses of promoting the Act is not known. But history is full of
cases where the small commoner who previously had the right to
graze a cow or a few sheep upon the common land, had to relin-
quish his share because of lack of funds. With nowhere to feed his
animals, he was obliged to sell out and either seek work in the towns
as a casual worker, or become a charge upon the parish poor-rates.

Muker, Keld, Reeth and Grinton common lands were enclosed
early in the 19th century. A glance at the higher slopes of the valley

will reveal the long straight walls enclosing land which was once common pasture. They radiate from the small irregular fields of the old enclosures, right up to the moor walls which shut out the heather-covered peaty wastes.

(1) In the County Record Office, Northallerton.
(2) This clause was probably inserted because, in a number of 18th century Enclosure Acts, Quakers were employed as surveyors or commissioners. The Quakers had by this time (1777) established their right to abstain from making oaths and making an affirmation instead.
(3) 7 quarter yards = 5 foot 3 ins.
(4) "coap" & "coble" are the two top layers of stone
(5) large stones binding the wall together.

A Tale of Two Chapels

BEFORE THE DISSOLUTION of the monasteries, there was a chapel at Keld, mentioned by Leland in 1530. It was closed following a riot of the inhabitants, which has never been fully explained. What put it into the heads of the people of Keld to work themselves up to such an extent as to desecrate their chapel, is hard to imagine. Amongst some old papers left by Anthony Clarkson of Smithyholme, Keld (1787-1847) is a piece of doggerel verse describing a most unusual affray, said to have taken place during a service at Keld chapel. Was this the story of the same "riot" passed down by word of mouth and then put into rhyme by Clarkson, three hundred years later?

This is the tale it tells. It was a hot Sunday morning in May. The chapel was full, and whilst the priest was praying — " ... that all might live in peace and harmony",

"There was a man that stood up in the place
Where he had sate and did proclaim 'Oyes!
Oyes! I want a calf, if any here
Can give me notice of one, far or near,
I duly will his labour recompense
And will for his trouble give him twopence'."

"Good words nor bad were spoken for a space
For each one held it a sad disgrace
That a Strainger should come hither and proclaim
This calf, our Holy House for to profane.
But each cried — 'I pray thee now begone
Or else we'll rive thy Flesh from off th' Bone'."

The rhyme goes on to say that upon his refusal to leave, they set on him to a man and the struggle got so involved that they began striking one another until the quarrel turned into a regular dog-fight. With black eyes and bleeding noses they fought amongst themselves. The noise attracted the attention of people outside the chapel, who came in and joined the fight, although not knowing what it was about. As the story goes:-

" ..... the like was never known before
For out of the Chapel went not one whole sark (shirt)
All was riven and torn one by one
Unless it was a lass that had none on."

The stranger who started the trouble slipped out, terrified, and was never seen again, but the place was so damaged and profaned that it never after was re-consecrated.

Keld chapel fell into ruins. The nearest place of worship was at Muker, and people living at the head of Swaledale had no church of their own for many a year.

In 1789, an Independent or Congregational minister, Edward Stillman, came to Swaledale. He first preached in a barn called Gun Ing cowhouse outside Muker. He had an attractive and commanding personality, had a powerful voice, and was an excellent singer. He was once asked to preach in Muker church, but he declined and held a meeting at the "Town gate" instead. After this he continued for more than two years to speak in cottages or farm-houses, from Muker to West Stonesdale.

One day, whilst at Keld, he was shown the ruins of the old chapel and the inhabitants promised to rebuild it, if he would stay amongst them. Standing in the centre of the ruins he accepted, and, planting his stick amidst the fallen debris, he said:

"Here will I have my chapel built, and here will I
preach the gospel."

Accordingly, a chapel and house were erected on the old site, at a cost of £700. Some of this money was raised locally, but most of it came from outside the dale. Stillman tramped from Keld to London and back, staying with friends on the way, begging for contributions. He walked over five hundred miles and collected £400, and his expenses were said to have been only sixpence.

Thus began a ministry which lasted forty-eight years and which greatly influenced the people of the upper dale. At his death in 1837, his place was taken by William Sedgwick who only stayed a year. Then came James Wilkinson, who was born at Beckside Farm, Howgill, near Sedbergh. He was a worthy successor to Edward Stillman. Having worked as a farmer in his youth, he was completely at home with his new congregation. He started a school and later organised the building of a literary institute. The latter cost £118 and one of the subscribers was James Backhouse, the Quaker naturalist and nurseryman of York. Wilkinson's ministry covered the period when increasing poverty, due to the slump in lead-mining, was causing much misery in the dale. His labours and anxieties over his various undertakings were the cause of his death in 1866 at the age of 61. But he left behind a chapel built upon a firm spiritual foundation and since then Keld and its neighbourhood have never been without its help and guidance.

A Wesleyan chapel built at Keld in 1841 was also the centre of a successful ministry.

The Corpse Way

CROSSING KISDON HILL between Keld and Muker, then fording the Swale and continuing up Iveletside, high up along the north slope of Swaledale, runs an ancient track which is now known as the "corpse-way". It was used by funeral parties when they carried their dead from the dale-head to a final resting place at the parish church of Grinton.

There is little doubt but that it is one of the oldest roads in the dale. Flint arrow-heads, found along its route, point to the fact that it was trodden by prehistoric man. The original path or "trod" avoided the wet marshy land in the valley bottom and the thick forest which covered the lower slopes. It follows the sunnier and warmer side of the dale, so it was natural that, when men came to settle in the valley of the Swale, they built their farms and hamlets on or near its course. Thus it became a link between one settlement and another.

Itinerant packmen, "badgers" and "higglers" journeying on foot or on ponies used it, carrying their wares of salt, corn and cloth. When lead-mining became the most important industry in the dale, it rang to the tread of the miners' clogs and the clopping of pony trains laden with smelted lead for Richmond and beyond. There were, of course, old bridle-ways on the other side of the valley. As the two sides were linked by "waths" or fords, these routes were probably used as alternative ways of getting to Grinton, depending largely upon the state of the river.

Dr. Whitaker, writing one hundred and fifty years ago, said that —

" ... before interments began to take place at Muker, the bodies of the dead were conveyed for burial upon men's shoulders upwards of twelve miles to the parish church, not in coffins but in rude wicker baskets."

As described above, funerals from Keld and Birkdale passed over Kisdon to Muker, but those from West Stonesdale, Frith, Smithyholme and Ravenseat kept to the left bank of the Swale and joined the "corpse-way" at Calvert Houses. Two pall-bearers were supplied from each of these hamlets in addition to the family bearers, so that the carrying could be done in relays.

Before the procession began, watch was kept over the body by each of the relatives in turn. Special biscuits and wine were handed over the wicker-coffin to the guests as they arrived. All the neighbours were "bidden" by personal calls, and sometimes as many as two hundred would attend the service. When a shepherd died a fleece of wool was placed in his coffin. His occupation could thus be proved on Judgment Day, so that his irregular attendance at church would be forgiven.

Whilst the journey down the dale lasted, the funeral guests lived at the expense of the bereaved. At intervals along the route, the body was laid upon stone slats or resting-stones, while the cortege halted for a while. There is still to be seen at the north approach to Ivelet Bridge a flat, elongated slab, which is pointed out as one of these old "coffin-stones". However, it may be argued that it owes its name not to the use made of it, but to its striking likeness to the shape of a coffin. In any case, Ivelet Bridge is not on the route of the so-called "corpse-way".

Travelling from the head of Swaledale to Grinton would take at least two days, depending upon the state of the weather. Funeral parties are said to have stayed the night at Feetham. Just above this village are the foundations of a building known as the "dead-house", where the wicker-coffins were left in safety whilst the procession slipped down to what is now the "Punch Bowl", to rest and refresh themselves. There is a tale told that once two funeral parties were using the wayside mortuary at the same time, and that it was only after the burial service had taken place, and when the effects of the "refreshment" had worn off, that the bearers realised that the bodies had been interred in the wrong graves.

As there were no bridges in the dale until the end of the six-teenth century, ponies were used to carry the wicker-coffins over the fords. Especially was this necessary when the rivers and becks were in spate. Many an accident must have occurred at this time, involving a bearer in a worse fate than just a wetting.

After the new chapel and burial ground at Muker were conse-crated in 1580, corpses from the dale-head and downwards as far as Gunnerside were carried to Muker; and those dying below Gunnerside continued to be taken on to Grinton as before. The custom of providing meat and drink for funeral parties continued. The "Queen's Head" at Muker, near the church, catered for them up to quite recent times. Here a sum of money called a "shot" was paid to the landlord by the dead person's relatives, to provide drinks to all the guests who called, until the "shot" was exhausted. They drank out of special "funeral mugs", which, when not in use, hung from the ceiling joists of the inn kitchen. When the "Queen's Head" was sold after the first world war and became a private house, the "gaily-decorated" mugs

61

were dispersed.

During the seventeenth century an Act of Parliament was passed, forbidding the use of linen shrouds or winding sheets, and ordering that the dead should be "buried in woollen". This was done in order to stimulate England's woollen cloth trade. The law was often evaded by the well-to-do, who gladly paid the statutory fine of five pounds. In fact, the continuance of the time-honoured custom of burying in linen almost became a licensed practice, the fine being regarded as a sort of fee, permitting the use of linen sheets.

The use of wicker carriers was certainly in vogue in 1716 when the curate of Muker gave notice that he would bury no more corpses without a coffin. Whether this ended the use of wicker baskets is not known. Heavier wooden coffins would certainly have made the journeys more arduous, and it is likely that sledges were used[1]. In 1828, William Hunter, aged 91, was drawn to his grave by his mare, aged 32.

Towards the end of the eighteenth century better roads were made; bridges were built by public subscription, and wheeled traffic began to supersede the old pack-horse trains. A hearse was bought by the township of Muker in 1836, a box-like structure on two wheels. The driver sat on a seat fixed to the front end, and the wheels were lined with leather to deaden their sound. On either side of the slightly domed roof were three black plumes or tassels. Sixpence was the usual fee for its use for persons residing in the Muker township, but outsiders paid sixpence a mile.

It was the custom to stop the cortege at the Muker school. The coffin was hauled out through the back of the hearse and lifted upon the shoulders of the pall-bearers; then, with the mourners chanting a dirge, the procession went up the village street to the church. Today the "corpse-way", with its tumbled stone walls, is a thing of the past, but visitors can still follow it on foot, undisturbed by traffic, which now keeps to the modern road along the valley bottom.

[1] sledges were used for farming purposes up to the middle of the present century.

Reeth in the Nineteenth Century

DURING THE EARLY PART of the last century, Reeth became
a town of some importance. It had had a chartered market since 1695
and livestock fairs took place there during the summer and autumn.
It was also for many years the centre of a prosperous lead-mining
industry. The population of Reeth reached its maximum in 1821, with
just under 1,500 inhabitants, nearly three times that of today. In
1841 it was still nearly 1,350.

The new "turnpike" road to Richmond was constructed in 1836,
and 12 years later Richmond station was opened for rail traffic. This
was a boon to the lead-mining interests. It also enabled the better-off
residents to obtain what was known as "station coal", which came
from the Durham coalfields. Previous to this, Swaledale folk had to be
satisfied with peat or the inferior coal from opencast pits near Tan
Hill, although one old lady said that she preferred the slow-burning
local fuel because "station coal sweated away fast". The cruel practice
of sending ten-year-old boys up the chimneys when they needed
cleaning was just as described in the novels of Dickens.[1]

Lighting was by tallow candles. Placed near each candle-stick
would be a pair of "snuffers", now antique curiosities, for putting
them out at night. Even the parson used one in his pulpit.

The outside appearance of the town houses has not altered
much. (By 1840 all the thatched roofs had been replaced by stone
slates). Internally however, there were no conveniences and very few
houses had piped water. Rainwater was collected from the roofs into
wooden tubs and, being "soft" water, was used on washing days.
Drinking water for the majority of people was carried from the two
pumps which stood on the "green" — one was known as the "Low"
Pump and stood next to Gill's ironmonger's shop. It had a pyramidal
roof, at the apex of which was a stone ball. It is now concreted over.

There were lively scenes at the Low Pump, especially on
Saturday nights when the residents queued-up for their Sunday
supplies of water. (Fetching it on the Sabbath day was unthinkable).
It was a natural meeting-place. The low wall which surrounded it at

that time made a convenient bench for gossiping and for playing "gundies" (or "five stones").

An interesting institution in the town was the "mangle house" where the women could have their washing mangled for a penny or two. There were always some young men hanging around, who were prepared to help with the turning of the handle, and, no doubt, matchmaking at the mangle was not unknown.

Lovers had their favourite walks on summer evenings. Such was Quaker Lane and down towards the Swale by the green lane, up Skellgate on to the moor, along the old Richmond road to Ewelop Hill, and through the Mill Ings crossing Arkle beck at the "hippings" (stepping-stones). And when darkness came, these places were said to be haunted by ghosts and hobgoblins whose mysterious noises made these evening walks all the more thrilling.

Market days, especially fair days, transformed the "green" into a crowded and animated scene. Long rows of butchers' stalls appeared on the cobbled pavement. Squealing piglets were kept in large canvas-covered casks. Young girls from Marske attended to the stalls of fruit and vegetables grown in their local gardens. Clothiers spread their wares on the grass. There were stalls for sweetmeats and spices; boots, clogs and pattens; ribbons, laces, gloves, handkerchiefs and galluses (braces). Knives, scissors, pans and "backstins", baskets, skeps, brushes, besoms and shigrams (shawls) were exposed for sale, in fact everything from a pin to a pig could be purchased.

Noisy haggling throngs of men, women and children surrounded the stalls. There was "Old Enos" with his famous Barnard Castle spices and Tom Lambert with his sweets and confectionery. If eating too many sweets gave one the toothache, down at the blacksmith's shop there was always a nice clean pair of pincers (or "nippers") kept ready for extractions.

The seven inns were open all day and as fair-days and market-days came to a close, the scene became noisier. Often some Irishmen or lead-miners would start fighting, but before things got completely out of hand the crowd would often intervene. The Irishmen would disappear to their cottages near the corn-mill, where some of them were employed. During this time the parish constable kept discreetly out of sight. He always turned a blind eye when the inns were emptied and their revellers staggered uncertainly into the streets. The constable was elected by the parishioners every two or three years. They usually chose the biggest man available, often the blacksmith. In his kitchen to impress the awe-striken youngsters, could be seen hanging his shining black enamelled and decorated baton and the brightly polished hand-cuffs, symbols of his office.

The seven inns in the 1840s were the "Black Bull", "King's

GRINTON
FEAST

SPORTINGS,

Will be held AUGUST 18th, 19th and 20th, 1873.

We, the official Stewards feel
Inclined thus humbly to appeal
To all who love hilarious sports—
Gymnastics of the nimblest sorts,
Athletics, frolics, recreations,
Enjoyments as on like occasions,—
With such circumgirations mix'd,
As will in proper turn be fix'd.

Our compliments we hereby send
To each true-hearted welcome friend,
Whose well-filled purses can augment
Our funds to be on pleasure spent.

Kind patronisers condescend
To visit, and assistance lend,
And all our sportings, never fear!
Shall equal ev'ry previous year,
Or else surpass, which we intend,
By making circumstances bend,
We purpose much, and hope that you
Will gladly help to carry through,
By lending your befriending aid
To cheer us in the efforts made.
We ask and hope you won't deny,
But cheerfully again comply.

Well-wishing public don't say 'nay!'
But join us on each festal day.

Unitedly, once more on earth,
Let Grinton ring with songs of mirth.

PRIZES.

Foot Race, 4s. for first, and 2s. for
  Second.

Pony Race for a Bridle.

Donkey Races for Bridles.

Dog Trails for a Kettle.

Pole Jumping for 3s.

Boy's Races for Caps.

Quoit Playing for a Teapot.

Jumping for Gloves.

Men and Boy's Three-Legged Race
  for a Hat.

Foot Race for 10s. 200 yards.

Waggoners' Race for a Whip.

And several other Prizes to be given

JOHN SCOTT AND RICHARD BIRKBECK, STEWARDS.

PHILLIPS AND CO. MACHINE PRINTERS, RICHMOND

The
Feast
xii   No 2

An 1873 handbill for Grinton Feast Sports.

Lead mining. Above: Faggergill miners, about 1900. Below: Weighing lead ingots at Richmond station about 1870.

The animal scene. Above: The Gunnerside smithy, with David Calvert, George Sunter and James Calvert. Below: Swaledale ewes on the moor, photographed by J.C. Moore.

The sound of music. Above: 'Neddy Dick' of Keld (Richard Alderson 1882 – 1926) with his percussion instrument made of stones taken from the river Swale. Below: Gunnerside Band outside its bandroom (the hipped roof building).

Arms", "King's Head", "Shoulder of Mutton", "Buck", "Red Lion"
and "Half Moon". Over the "Half Moon" kitchen was the savings bank
in the charge of Dick, Quaker Thompson's son, who acted as agent
or clerk. Dick's father was the schoolmaster at the Quaker school.[2]

A rudimentary type of education, mainly devoted to the learning
of reading, writing, arithmetic and singing, was carried on by the three
schools, viz: the grammar school at Fremington, the Wesleyan school
in Reeth and the Quaker school in the back lane. Education in those
days was not compulsory and attendances were most irregular, mainly
owing to bad weather and the demand for labour when hay-making,
peat-cutting and drying, and sheep-washing took place. Truancy was
also frequent, especially on fair days and when circuses came to town.
The children were thrilled to see the tight-rope dancers and when the
performers left, the young folk would try to imitate what they had
seen, but with little success.

The scholars at the Fremington school celebrated Shrove Tuesday
by locking the master out, and when he tried to enter, they sang in
chorus the following — "Pardon Master, Pardon Master, Pardon! If you
don't give us a holiday we'll never let you in" etc. The master evidently
took it all in good part. At the Gunnerside National School, the master
made the following entry in his log-book:-

"1863 May 29th: Allowed the scholars to go home early:
they sent me the following note:- 'Dear Sir, If you please will
you let us have a holiday this afternoon as it is the Royal Oak
day in remembrance of our King, Charles I, who hid in an
oak-tree when his enemies were in search of him. We remain etc.
schoolboys of Melbecks National School, Gunnerside'."

They tried it on the following year, but as May 29th fell upon
a Sunday, permission was not granted.

At all these village schools, the sons of miners left at ten years
of age and accompanied their fathers to the lead-mines, where they
were set to work upon the least arduous jobs. A substantial number
of dales children, however, did stay at school long enough to be able
to read, and it was probably they, when they grew up, who patronised
the literary institutes and libraries which were being established in
all the larger villages.

In 1826, George Peacock, son of the Wesleyan Minister, wrote a
parody of the lives of some of Reeth's prominent citizens. At that
time Reeth could boast of its rhymesters and musicians. John Stubbs,
a local preacher, published a volume of original tunes. There was also
Thomas Coates, a writer of humorous satire who kept the Post Office.

Rhyming seems to have been prevalent in Reeth for many
years. In Bulmer's North Riding Directory for 1890, under the
heading "shopkeepers" of Reeth, appears the name of Jabez Raisbeck,

"printer and stationer, bookseller and agent for the 'Darlington and Stockton Times'." He was reputed to have been a writer of poetry. In order to furbher his poetic ambition, and whenever his business would allow, he escaped to the top of Fremington Edge. Here he had found a natural cavity in the cliff. Having added a protecting wall and other additional comforts to it, he used to sit there writing his verses, far removed from the bustling life of Reeth. The place is marked on the Ordnance map as "Jabez Cave".

(1) The use of boy sweeps was abolished in 1875.
(2) See "The History of Reeth Friends' School" (E. Cooper), 1970.

Captain John Harland

JOHN HARLAND (1788-1875) fought for his country in the
Napoleonic wars. He lived at one time at Marrick but spent most of
his 87 years at Reeth.[1] He gave a great deal of his time to the
welfare of his neighbours. He was a member of the Board of Guardians
of the Reeth Union and was in close touch with the Commissioners
of the Poor Law, when the new Amendment Act came into force in
1834. This Act abolished the old parish relief system and placed the
responsibility for the maintenance of the poor upon the newly created
Poor-law Unions[2], thereby spreading the cost of relief over a wider
area.

We first hear of Captain Harland in the winter of 1821-2, when
enormous snowdrifts blocked the old Richmond road, making it
impassable for many days. To relieve the beleaguered inhabitants of
Reeth, he organized a gang of 114 volunteers, who, "using beef suet
to grease their spades", cut a way through the snow in the direction
of Marske.

Captain Harland was a man of some literary ability. He compiled
a glossary of Swaledale dialect words which was later published by the
English Dialect Society in 1873, when he was over 80 years old. He wil
be remembered chiefly for his poem of "Reeth Bartle Fair", which
recalls in vigorous verse memories and humours of an annual fair on St.
Bartholomew's Day, when the lead-miners spent freely their hard-earnec
wages and forgot the monotony of their lives.

REETH BARTLE FAIR

This mworning as I went to wark,
I met *Curly* just cumman heeam;
He had on a new flannin sark,
An he saw 'at I'd just gitten'd t'seeam.
'Whar's te been?' sed awd Curly to me;
'I've been down to Reeth Bartle Fair.'
'Swat[3] te down, mun, sex needles',[4] sed he,
'An tell us what seets te saw thar.'

67

'Wya,[5] t'lads all ther best shun[6] had put on,
An t' lasses donn'd all ther best cwoats;
I saw five pund of Scotch wether mutton
Sell'd by *Ward* and *Tish Tom* for five grwoats.
Bowlaway had fine cottons to sell;
Butteroy lace an hankutchers[7] browt;
Young *Tom Cwoats* had a stall tuv his-sel,
An had ribbins for varra near nowt.

Thar was *Enos* had good brandy-snaps,[8]
Bill Brown as good spice[9] as cud be;
Potter Robin an mar syke-like chaps
Had t' bonniest pots te cud see;
John Ridley and awd *Willy Walls,*
An *Naylor*, and twea or three mar,
Had apples and pears at ther stalls,
An *Gardener Joe* teaa was thar.

Thar was sizzors an knives an reaad purses,
An plenty of awd cleeathes o' t' nogs;[10]
An tweea or three awd spavin'd horses,
An plenty of shun an new clogs.
Thar was plenty of gud iron pans,
An pigs 'at wad fill all t' deeale's hulls;
Thar was baskets and skeps an tin cans,
An bowls, an wood thivles for gulls.

Thar was plenty of all macks o' meeat,
An plenty of all sworts o' drink;
An t' lasses gat monny a treeat,
For t' gruvers[11] war all full o 'chink.[12]
I cowp'd [13] my black hat for a white in;
Lile Jonas had varra cheeap cleeath;
Jem Peacock and *Tom* talk'd o' feightin',
But *Gudgeon Jem Puke* [14] lick'd 'em beeath.

Thar was dancing an feightin' forever;
Will Wade sed 'at he was quite grieved;
An *Pedlety* tell'd 'em hee'lt never
Forgit 'em as lang as he lieved.
They knock'd yan another about,
Just warse than a sham to be seen;
Charlie Will luk'd as white as a clout,
Kit Puke gat a pair o' black een.

I spied our awd lass in a nuke,
Drinkan shrub wi' grim *Freesteeane*, fond lad.
I gav her a varra grou luke,
O, connies, but I was just mad.
Seea I went to *John Whaites's* to drink,
Whar I war'd tweea an seeumpins[15] i' gin;
I knaw not what follow'd, but think
I'd paddled through 't muck thick an thin.

For to-day, when I gat out o' bed,
My cleeathes wer all sullied sea sar;
Our Peggy and all our fwoak sed
To Reeth Fair I sud never gang mar;
But it's rake-time, seea I mun away,
For my partners are all g'yan to wark:' —
Seea I lowp'd up an bad him gud day,
An wrowt at t' Awd Gang [16] tell 't was dark.

---

[1] Harland House lies north-east of the "green".

[2] Reeth Union formed 1840.

[3] Squat. [4] A common phrase, signifying an interval during which a woman knitting would work the loops off 'six needles.' [5] Well. [6] Shoes.
[7] Handkerchiefs. [8] Small cakes of ginger-bread. [9] Ginger-bread.
[10] Wooden pegs. [11] Miners. [12] Money. [13] Exchanged, bartered, swapped.
[14] A change from the surname 'Peacock' to distinguish a particular family or branch. [15] Spent 2s. 7d. [16] The name of a lead mine.

The Decline of the Lead Mining Industry

THE YEAR 1830 was marked by great distress throughout
Swaledale, due to a drop in the price of lead and to bad results in
agriculture. With wages reduced to almost starvation level, large
numbers of miners and their families left to seek their fortunes elsewhere. Many sailed for America, where some found work near
Dubuque, a lead-mining area on the banks of the Mississippi, in what
later became part of the State of Iowa.

The first to settle there appear to have been John Bell and
Richard Waller from Whitaside. John Bell eventually started a whole-
sale dry-goods store in Dubuque and did well. Richard Waller and his
brother Robert who had followed him, in partnership with Richard
Bonson, made fortunes by constructing blast-furnaces for smelting
lead-ore. Scores of dalesmen, both farmers and miners, followed the
pioneers' example and settled in the same district. There was James
Hammond from Reeth, who eventually farmed three hundred acres
and bred shorthorns. Richard Spensley, also from Reeth, was said
to have kept up his Swaledale dialect until his death in 1892 aged
88. On the other hand those who stayed at home faced unemployment and many became a charge upon the Poor Law institutions.
Others found temporary employment on the railway lines which were
being constructed at that time, or drifted into the coal-mining
industry in Durham or into the cotton mills of Lancashire.

The people who organized the Reeth Fair and Cattle Show which
took place on 3rd November, 1848, were obviously worried by the
plight of the miners. As well as offering the usual premiums for the
best agricultural exhibits, the programme began with the following
competitive item:-

> "A premium of £2 to the working miner of good char-
> acter who has brought up the greatest number of children to
> the age of ten years without parochial assistance."

After the show "a large party partook of a sumptuous dinner
provided at the Buck Inn". The "working-miners" were not present
at this entertainment, perhaps because there was no one whose

character was acceptable to the organizers.

Attempts were made about 1850 to revive the lead-mining industry, and met with partial success. Machinery was introduced for crushing, riddling and washing the ore, for driving the bellows in the smelt mills, and for pumping out accumulations of water. But all this was expensive and increased the cost of production. Then came, about 1870, increasing competition from foreign lead-mines, chiefly in Italy and Spain, so that mining in Swaledale became an uneconomic proposition. One by one the companies went into liquidation or transferred their activities elsewhere. The Hurst and Grinton mines were partially closed in 1880, causing several large families to leave the dale. Some went to find work in the woollen mills at Keighley and others to the cotton mills of Burnley, Nelson and Colne. In 1890 the Hurst mines finally closed, but the industry which had lasted 1,800 years lingered on until about 1920.

The Condition of the Poor

TO WHAT EXTENT the poorer section of the community had suffered as a result of the closing down of the monastic houses (1538-9) it is impossible to judge with any certainty. At that time, the hungry could usually count upon some "broken meats" and scraps at the gates of the monasteries, and this unorganised and indiscriminate system of relief was common to all the religious houses in England. Beggars and mendicants, hungry and ill-clothed, roamed the countryside before the dissolution, but afterwards their numbers increased greatly. This terrible state of affairs continued until the end of Queen Elizabeth's reign.

In order to mitigate these conditions, a law was passed in 1601, making each parish responsible for alleviating the distress of its own poor. This duty was entrusted to the churchwardens, or Select Vestry as it was later called. It was usually made up of 24 members. This committee was empowered to fix a poor rate, the amount being subject to the approval of the Justices of the Peace. Two overseers, appointed annually, as well as a salaried constable and a vestry clerk, were responsible for the collection of the poor rate or "cess". They organised its distribution in the form of pensions for the aged and disabled, the upkeep of a poor-house, the provision of food and clothing for the destitute, the obtaining and enforcement of affiliation orders in bastardy cases, and other matters affecting the wellbeing of the inhabitants.

The recipients of relief were called "paupers". Paupers had no individual rights. They were entitled to get relief only from the parish in which they were born, or in which they were legally settled. Wanderers from other parishes in search of work were looked upon with suspicion and steps were taken to have them removed.

The following are a few examples recorded in the church-warden's account books of Muker illustrating the procedure:-

    1744   "For sheeften (shifting) Christopher Spade and
           his wife — 5s 6d — for a Brief[1] — 1s 6d"

<table>
<tr><td>1823</td><td>"Jan. 22nd. Resolved that a woman now in the township shall be taken to the Magistrate by the Constable on Tuesday next."</td></tr>
<tr><td>1828</td><td>"Feb. 5th. Resolved that owing to a woman, her name unknown, stopping in the Township of Muker, the opinion of an Attorney will be taken the first opportunity in order to know how the said woman must be disposed of."</td></tr>
</table>

In most cases people in distress were given food, footwear, clothing and monetary relief. When William Bell applied for relief to the Arkengarthdale Select Vestry[2], he was given "a pair of clogs, a pair of trousers, a shirt, a pair of stockings and a smock frock." The same Vestry allowed Matthew Pepper's wife a pair of clogs and a supply of bread with the stipulation that her daughter must work for Matthew Chalder, a member of the Vestry.

Arkengarthdale had other problems in 1819 — "Whereas various complaints have been made against several wanton and disorderly persons, who make practice of gaming and doing mischiefs on the Sabbath day, we the undersigned, being the minister, churchwardens and select vestry, do the utmost in our power to put a stop to such practices for the future, by suspending all pensions from those who are paupers, as well as dismissing from our employ all persons of whatevver description who are employed to work for any of us, without paying any respect to any who are found guilty, until they make due submission and promise not to do the like again and also attend church for three successive Sundays,without a reasonable excuse for every time a complaint is made against them."

This warning was not completely effective, for in February, 1831, when John Chalder applied for a continuation of his 13s a week pension, the Vestry "ordered that 6s 6d a week be stopped him for a fortnight on account of his sons gaming on the Sabbath day, hunting at night and throwing people's fences down".

John Rycroft applied for bread but this was refused and further he lost his job because he threatened his employer "that he would knock his brains out" for persuading the Vestry to deduct 2s from his pension as he was neglecting his work.

Again the Vestry ordered — "that Edward Peacock's pension be stopped till such times as he cleans the road from Arkle town to Toll Bar, if he only works one hour in the day."

Amongst the minutes of the Muker Vestry meetings are the following:-

    1824 — Feb. 4th "Resolved that Joss Coates, widow, of Keld shall sell her clock or any other superfluous furniture if she cannot do with her present pension."

1824 — Dec. 29th "Resolved that the chest of drawers etc.
belonging to Isabel Buckle shall be sold by public
auction next week."

And so it was decided in 1831, that the payment of a pension
might be made only on the condition that the pauper had no superfluous possessions, the meanest of "means tests"! All pensioners
were visited and all their goods and furniture which were deemed
unnecessary were collected and auctioned for the benefit of the
pension fund and the ratepayers.

Some people living in the township of Muker resented this
interference with the property of the poor. A rhyme was found in
the parish chest, written by someone who sympathised with the
pensioners. Some of the verses are given below:-

"Lines written in consequence of that most infernal plot in the
Parish of Muker, made in order to deprive the paupers of all
that furniture which the Parish Officers thought to be
unnecessary, and selling them by public auction on that most
memorable day — Muker Fair, January 4th, 1832."

Come all honest men who have cesses to pay
Let your care be attention to what I shall say.
Your wise Vestry Laws, restrictions and rules
Are left to a parcel of asses and fools.

Nay worse than all that the intent upon evil.
Their works prove they are in league with the Devil.
These human infernals, their masters surpass
In planning out evil while drinking the glass[3].

Yet who could have thought it could enter their brains
As only such men as had hold of the reins.
This business most surely has hatched in hell
To take from the paupers, their prayer books to sell.

Old Nick was diverted their tricks to behold
While gathering the trapsticks, or heaps, to be sold
And Renny that sly fox along with his cub[4]
Seized hold of their fury, the poor people to rob.

These hard-hearted monsters pursuing their plan
Seized clocks, sir, and cupboards and frying-pan,
Fire-irons, hand-irons, kitchen table and all,
With various articles they made up the whole.

'Tis strange, sir, indeed, that all these wiseacres
Themselves should demean, and so be partakers.

Churchwardens and members of Vestry combine
To accomplish an object that was not divine.

Did ere such a case as the present occur
All men in their senses, must surely demur.
None ever before this, beheld such a sight
Where the poor by the rich were robbed of their right.

Such sinners as these may shake hands and agree
To ease the poor people of their property.
On Tommy they fix, as the most proper man
To bring to perfection this horrible plan.

On such an excursion, with two or three more
They did such an act, as was ne'er done before.
'Tis hoped such another will not be again
So long as the Parish of Muker remain.

The Muker parish registers tell us something about the incidence
of pauperism. During the 10 year period 1785 - 1794 the parish clerk,
when recording burials, besides giving the persons'occupations, also
stated which ones died as paupers. From this record we arrive at the
following table:-

Year	Total Number of Burials	Number of Paupers	No. of Paupers who were Miners, or Children & Wives of same
1785	22	3	2
1786	20	9	6
1787	50	22	18
1788	51	12	8
1789	44	19	13
1790	38	23	22
1791	38	17	12
1792	28	8	6
1793	37	13	10
1794	42	17	13
Totals	370	143	110

Thus 38.6% of deaths occurring during these years were those of
persons receiving parish relief, and 76.9% of the latter were miners or
their wives and children. There was indeed a great amount of poverty
during the years 1785-1794 but in the 1830s and the "hungry
forties" conditions were probably just as bad, if not worse. Between
1830 and 1840 serious unemployment occurred in the lead-mining

industry and hundreds were thrown out of work. The Overseers of the
Swaledale and Arkengarthdale parishes were at their wits' ends,
endeavouring to meet the needs of the workless. The ratepayers, too,
were finding it difficult to accept the demands for increased assessments.
In 1830, the total relief bill for the Muker parish had reached nearly
£1,000 per annum. It was stated in the Vestry minutes that there was
very little employment in the district "except knitting, the mines
being exhausted". But in this pitiful state of things Swaledale was no
exception. Bad harvests and increased living costs prevailed generally
in the English countryside and towns.

In 1834, the Poor Law Amendment Act was passed. The purpose
of this was to abolish outdoor relief and to unite parishes into large
units, so that paupers could be concentrated into workhouses where
the elderly, the infirm and the children could reside, and where able-
bodied beggars and tramps could receive temporary accommodation
and food, in exchange for a certain amount of menial work, such as
stone-breaking or gardening. The whole point of the Act was to make
life in a workhouse less attractive than employment in field and
factory[5].

It was originally intended that the Swaledale parishes should be
part of an area centred upon Richmond, and in fact the Richmond
Union was formed in 1837. This new arrangement caused great
opposition in the dale and pleas were submitted to the Poor Law
Commissioners asking to be independent. The reasons given for this
were (a) that the dale industry was mostly lead-mining and therefore
had very different problems from those of the agricultural area
around Richmond; and (b) that parishes in Swaledale and Arkengarthdale were so far from Richmond, that the dalesfolk would be placed
at a disadvantage. After many meetings being held with the Assistant
Commissioners, the latter agreed to split the area, and the Reeth
Union was formed in 1840.

Muker parish actually attempted to keep its own independence
and refused, at first, to produce its poor-law books. It submitted later
to the new arrangement, after being told that it would be allowed to
elect a guardian, and that its action might lead to fines and to the
imprisonment of its overseers and churchwardens.

The Reeth Poor Law Union eventually comprised the parishes
of Arkengarthdale, Ellerton Abbey, Grinton, Marrick, Melbecks,
Muker and Reeth. In 1851, there were 137 paupers in the Union,
being 2% of the total population. Of these, 108 were receiving outdoor relief in the form of pensions, 23 resided in the Reeth Union
Workhouse[6], and six in the pre-union poor-houses. Most of the 23
inmates were unmarried mothers with their illegitimate children;

the others were elderly or unemployed men and women. Although the new Act was intended to abolish outdoor relief, the more humane treatment of the poor was continued in the dale and enabled the paupers to stay in their own homes or live with relatives. The accommodation in the Reeth workhouse in 1890 was intended for 34 inmates but only 18 were actually in residence.[7] Poor people were haunted by the idea that they might end their days in the workhouse: there was a stigma attached to residing there.

In 1843, J.W. Harland of Marrick replied to enquiries made by the Assistant Poor Law Commissioners regarding the employment and condition of women and children living in the parish of Marrick. He estimated that about one-third of the women worked out of doors, preferring it to indoor work. From October to February, the principal employment for women was the pulling of turnips for which they earned 8d per day; March to June, weeding, for 10d a day; and July to September, hay-making and reaping, for 1/- a day. Women undertaking lead-ore washing earned 1/- a day. Working hours were usually eight daily, except during hay-making, when ten hours were expected. Their meals consisted of tea before going out at 7 a.m; bread and milk, or a little fried bacon and potatoes for dinner from 12 noon to 1 p.m., and for supper, tea or bread and milk. Harland emphasised that outdoor employment did not injure the manners and morals of girls of 15 or upwards, but those having no outdoor employment or regular domestic work tended to become indolent.

Knitting frocks and stockings was the main occupation, which earned women about 4d a day. Some families were granted allotments of a quarter to half an acre rent-free. These were dug usually by women and children, and were well cultivated. Such allotments invariably fostered habits of industry and improved the condition of families occupied in this way. Benefit or clothing clubs were encouraged and were on the increase. As to health, bronchial and pulmonary affections were the most common ailments, but this was attributed by Harland to the nature of the climate. Rents varied between 30/- and £3 per annum. The cottages generally consisted of two rooms and a pantry, both being inconvenient and ill-ventilated.

Children by nine years old had usually learnt to read and write, and they began work from that age onwards. The boys accompanied their fathers to the lead mines. Others were employed in farm work and their working hours were six in the mines or eight in the fields, for which they earned about 6d a day. Their diet consisted of bread and milk or hasty pudding (oatmeal). Boys working out of doors kept on the whole in good health, but those who worked in the mines sometimes became asthmatic. Girls were usually employed in knitting.

In 1841, J.W. Harland reported on the mining industry. To begin with, an enquiry was made in each parish, to ascertain the average duration of life of the mining population during the seven years 1835 - 1841. It was found that:-

In Marrick   15 miners died, average age 45.6 years
In Arkengarthdale   70 miners died, average age 45.5 years
In Muker   39 miners died, average age 45.7 years
and in Grinton (including
Reeth and Melbecks)   40 miners died, average age 55.0 years

this being a total of 164 with an average age at death of about 48. This is not of course what an actuary would call a real mortality experience, because the average age at death of all births recorded would be much lower.

The condition of the miners in 1841 is well chronicled in a letter written by J.W. Harland to Sir I. Waltham, Bt., one of the Poor Law Commissioners, as follows:-

"The prevailing diseases throughout the whole district are bronchial affections and rheumatism which may generally be attributed to cold and rain after leaving the close warm atmosphere of the mine.

The miners' dwellings in Marrick are generally small thatched cottages, situated very near their work. They are consequently less exposed to wet and cold on their way home. But although dry and kept tolerably clean, from want of room and proper ventilation the inmates are more liable to contagious disorders than the more comfortably lodged miners in the Parish of Grinton.

In Arkendale (Arkengarthdale) the houses are of a some-what better description, but the drainage imperfect, the habits of the people intemperate and filthy — cutaneous disorders very common. They are frequently victims of typhus and other malignant fevers. In the Parish of Grinton, including Reeth and Melbecks, the houses are of a decidedly superior description. Forty years ago they were mostly thatched with Ling or Heath. Thatch has now almost entirely disappeared. The population are comfortably lodged, generally well clothed, clean and orderly in their habits, and I have no doubt to these causes may be attributed the great difference between the mortality of this Parish and that of Arkendale.

In Muker the mortality in proportion to its population is nearly the same as in Arkendale, but many of the miners work occasionally in coal mines — are more exposed to storms by reason of their work being at a greater distance from their dwellings — and these dwellings also of a description inferior to those of the other townships within the Parish of Grinton.

From these circumstances, I infer that the average duration of a lead miner's life and his greater freedom from disease have increased in proportion to the increased airiness and increased convenience of his dwelling.

I have only to add that (with a few exceptions in Muker) every miner in this district sleeps in his own house."

[1] a writ or summons.
[2] Darlington & Stockton Times. "Arkengarthdale Records".
[3] Meetings of the Select Vestry were held at one of the Inns.
[4] William Raynard. Clerk to the Vestry.
[5] "English Social History" G.M. Trevelyan. 1944.
[6] This was situated on the south side of the village green, below the Congregationalist Church and behind Audrey's hair-dressing establishment, which was then the workhouse lodge.
[7] Bulmer's 1890 Directory of the North Riding.

Carriers, Turnpike roads and Railways

UNTIL THE BEGINNING of the last century pack-ponies were used for all carrying purposes. Lead ingots were taken to Barnard Castle, Stockton and Yarm in specially made panniers fitted to the backs of ponies. Both horses and donkeys were used on the farm for all transport work.

About 1820 the road system of Britain was being revolutionised by the methods introduced by John Macadam[1]. In 1836 a "macadamised" turnpike road was constructed from Grinton to Richmond along the valley bottom. The old toll-bar cottage still exists near Haggs Gill, where drivers of vehicles and ponies paid the charges towards the cost and upkeep of the new road, and also towards the dividends to those who had invested in the project, for turnpike roads were privately financed.

In 1840, there were three carriers from Reeth. John Close's conveyance left every Saturday morning with passengers, parcels and produce for Leeds, arriving there late on Monday evening and starting the return journey on Tuesday evening, and home again on Thursday night. Edward Close carried to Richmond and back every Saturday and David Alderson did the same to Barnard Castle every Wednesday.

In 1845, J.H. Robinson, butter factor and carrier, plied a "superior weekly conveyance by sprung wagon" to Leeds by way of Leyburn, Middleham, Masham, Ripon and Harrogate. He made a quicker journey than John Close, leaving Reeth at 7 a.m. every Wednesday, and getting home again on Saturday evening. These scheduled journeys helped dalespeople to overcome the disadvantages of having no railway up the dale. On 10th September, 1848, a branch line was opened connecting Richmond with the York, Newcastle and Berwick Railway at Eryholme Junction, later to become part of the North Eastern Railway Company's system. Richmond station then became the main depot for the lead ingots which were carried there from the smelting mills in wagons along the newly constructed turnpike road.

The rapid expansion of the railways in the north of England during the 1840s was the envy of those engaged in the lead-mining industry. It was tantalising that the railway should stop at Richmond. In 1863, hoping to get their products more easily and rapidly to the markets, a group of mine-owners and lessees held a meeting at the Buck Inn, Reeth, when it was proposed to form a company to build and maintain a railway up Swaledale, to be known as the Richmond and Reeth Railway Company. A brief budget was prepared by an engineer showing the cost of driving a line as far as Reeth and the purchasing of rolling-stock for a total sum of £35,000. Eventually a contractor named Hutchinson agreed to construct a line for £8,500 in cash plus an allotment of £15,000 in debentures and £12,500 in ordinary shares. The cost of engines and rolling-stock was estimated at £2,000. The promoters asked the North Eastern Railway Company to help finance the construction, but they would only promise to give working facilities when the line had been built, and as local financial support was insufficient the scheme was dropped.

In 1881 a Mr. Myers produced a plan for a line to run right up Swaledale as far as Muker, where it would tunnel one and three-quarter miles under Muker Common and Shunnor Fell and so to Hawes. The "Commoners of Muker and Thwaite" gave their consent, and Francis Garth of Crackpot was sent to interview the directors of the N.E.R., but they were not interested.

The last attempt to have a rail connection with Richmond was made in 1912. James William Close tried to form a light railway with a terminus at Fremington. It was to leave Richmond station along the south bank of the Swale, but when it reached the steep slopes of Billy Bank wood, the plan was to cross a loop in the river bed which would have involved the building of two bridges within a hundred yards or so of each other. Back again to the south bank it was to be carried on for another four miles, and then over another bridge to the north bank via Marrick Abbey to Fremington. The terminus at Fremington was to be sited in the corner of the field near Draycott Hall, at the junction of the Marske road, just 10 miles from Richmond. Local enthusiasm waxed high when the Reeth Rural District Council offered to help with a loan of £10,000 but when the final estimate of costs was worked out the council got "cold feet" and withdrew its offer. And so it ended. The first World War came and no more was heard of a Swaledale railway.

---

[1] John L. Macadam (1756-1836). His road-making consisted of layers of broken stones of uniform size, each layer being separately crushed into position by traffic or, later on, by heavy rollers.

Cricket in the Dale

UP TO THE MIDDLE of the last century sporting events were confined to shooting over dogs, fox-hunting with beagles, bare-fisted boxing, cock-fighting, horse-riding and wrestling. But towards the end of this period, cricket became popular. Who introduced the game into Swaledale will probably never be known. The issue of the "Wensleydale Advertiser" of August 19th, 1844, reported that —

" ... a friendly game of cricket was played at Grinton between eleven of the Grinton and Marrick Club and eleven of the Leyburn United Club, the latter coming off victorious with thirty notches[1] to spare."

On 2nd September of the same year, the Swaledalers journeyed to Leyburn for a return match which resulted in a draw. Leyburn scored 28 and 34. Bulmer was top scorer in both innings, getting 5 and 9 respectively, while W. and J. Langstaff took most of their wickets. Grinton and Marrick made 34 and 28. W. Langstaff, getting 15 "notches" in the first innings, was out "body before wicket" for 3 in the second innings. After the match the players adjourned to the "Oak Tree Inn" and had an excellent dinner, spending the evening "in cheerful conviviality".

In September 1848, the Grinton eleven crossed over into Wensley-dale and beat a combined eleven from Redmire, Preston and Bolton, by an innings and 24 "notches". On the Grinton side J. Blenkiron scored 27 and J. Alderson was not out 27. D. Hodgson took 13 wickets. The scores were Grinton 81 and Redmire etc. 32 and 25. One can imagine the return of the high-spirited victors as they galloped their ponies home along the Grinton moor road in the light of a September moon.

---

(1) runs were counted by cutting notches on a stick.

A Swaledale Smithy

FROM THIS DISTANCE in time we are apt to forget what a variety of activities went on in dales' villages 100 years ago. The present-day manufacture of standardised and factory-made everyday utensils has taken from the countryside a great deal of its independence and its sense of creation. The dexterity with which the village craftsman could turn his hand to anything with skill and ingenuity is something which we greatly miss. The village saddler, shoe-maker, weaver, dyer, tailor, carpenter and even the blacksmith are now almost extinct. They were once active partners with those engaged in agriculture, each a complement to the other. A few old men still carry on some of these dying trades, relics of an age when people took a pride in work well done.

Occasionally one still finds a blacksmith's shop open which has been owned and run through the generations from father to son. One peeps inside and sees the usual heaps of rusty iron, worn-out horse-shoes, pieces of old implements, which in former times would be used sooner or later, for making something new.

But the blacksmith no longer makes scythes and hooks, hoes hammers, picks, spades and mattocks — these can all be bought at the ironmongers in the nearest town. This also applies to all the domestic wants of the countryside. Clogs are now rarely worn and therefore "carkering of clogs"[1] is no longer done. Iron pots and pans which, if kept repaired, would last for ever, have given place to aluminium ware. The old-fashioned baking ovens have been replaced by electric and other patent cookers. Admittedly, work in the homes and farms have been lightened by modern inventions, but at the loss of those specialised craftsmen who contributed so much to the life of the countryside.

Turning over the leaves of the Gunnerside blacksmith's account book of 1840, one is forced to think of this revolution in our way of life. Most of the ledger entries refer to making horse-shoes and "carkering clogs" but there are, as well, hundreds of other items relating to everyday needs. Some of these written in the dale's dialect are given below:-

BUCKER mending — a bucker was a heavy piece of iron with a wooden shaft or handle fitted, which was used to break millstone grit into sand for sprinkling house floors; and also for crushing lead-ore.

CRUKE for bacon — Cruke was used for any kind of hook.

new FORMELD scythe — Formeld meant "made to order".

GITH for pig-tub — Gith, the metal band or hoop surrounding a wooden tub.

LIMER Mending — Limer, the shaft of a cart.

LUG for pail — Lug, a handle.

NOOK STOURS or STOWERS for peat cart — iron-work slots into which cart sides were fixed to enlarge its carrying capacity.

NIBS HOUPING — securing handles or "ribs" to a scythe.

NIPERS mending — pincers.

PLEUFE irons sharpening — Pleufe, a plough

STUBBING HACK sharpening — a mattock.

Churn SWAPE mending — Swape, a handle.

4 lb. STUBBS — old and used horse-shoe nails.

SHANDY wheel hooping and nailing — Shandy, a covered-in two-wheel cart.

TENTER CRUKES repairing — hooks used for stretching cloth on a frame, i.e. "tenter hooks".

new handle for SKELLET — Skellet, a saucepan.

SHECKLE for cow-band — Sheckle, a swivel.

new bars and loups to screw into SOWKER STONE for RECKINS to hinge on — a sowker-stone was the broad flagstone let into the chimney-breast, into which was fixed the metal bar for suspending 'reckin'' irons to support kettles, pans, etc.

GAVELOCK mending — a crow-bar.

JUMPERS sharpening — drills (for lead-miners).

Making GITH and handles for making DOLLY-TUB — Dolly-tub was until recently the name for a peggy-tub or wash-tub.

Pin and links for ENDHECK — an endheck was the rack containing fodder for the horse, swung at the back of a cart or waggon.

BRANDRITH mending — a trivet or metal base for supporting a kettle or pan, sometimes fixed to fire-bars and other times raised on three legs to rest upon the hearth.

Washers for KELP or KILP — an iron hook in the chimney on which pots are hung, a detachable handle of a metal pot, or miner's waggon chains.

RINDER — a tapering auger; a tool used for bevelling the sides of a round hole.

Hesp and staple for SNUBER — Snuber, a piece of wood with iron at the ends reaching across the shafts of a cart to prevent the cart from tipping up.

RIDSTAKE — the stake to which cattle are bound in the stalls.
STILIONS and TROUNS mending — parts of a steel-yard or balance
for weighing.
For most repairs only a few pence were charged. A hay-fork
could be made for two shillings, a horse-shoe made and fitted
for sixpence, a scythe for six shillings and a new range with
turn-bar cost one pound.

(Acknowledgements are due to the late Mr. W.H. Calvert of Gunnerside
who, with his father and grandfather before him, kept the Gunnerside
smithy).

---

(1) "Carkering" — the nailing of "carkers", strips of iron the shape of both sole
and heel to wooden clog bottom.

Farming in the Dale

IF ARTHUR YOUNG had been able to pay another visit to the northernmost Yorkshire Dales a century later, he would have been able to tell a different story. From Brough he would have found a road, no longer a "dreadful" track, but one suitable for wheeled traffic.

Early in the nineteenth century, a "turnpike" road was constructed from Reeth up Arkengarthdale to just beyond the "C.B." Inn where a toll-bar cottage stood. Market carriers were plying weekly over the Stang to Barnard Castle. Young would have noticed the flocks of black-faced sheep grazing upon the rough pastures and moorland from Tan Hill to Calver Hill. In addition to the tiny hamlets of Whaw, Langthwaite, Arkletown and Booze, neat farm-houses were dotted upon the hill-sides on the newly enclosed pastures which were formerly commons and waste. As the valley descended to Reeth, more and more green meadows occupied each side of Arkle Beck.

Young would have approved of at least one farmer, who, followed by his son, kept a record of all his buying and selling from 1875 to 1945. These day-book entries give one a picture of progress made during two generations; a small selection of them are given. The prices obtained for "wether" lambs[1] at the autumn sales fetched, with very little fluctuation, between 9s. and 15s. each until the 1914-18 war. Then came a sudden upward trend soaring to 47s. 6d. in 1920. From that date the prices as quickly dropped until 1932, during the "years of depression", to as low as 9s. each. Prices rose a little in the late thirties averaging between 18s. and 19s. a lamb, until wartime controls took over in 1940 and animals were sold at so much a pound.

Wool sales showed a decline from 8¾d. a pound in 1875 to 3½d. a pound in 1901, probably due to the increasing imports of this commodity from Australia and New Zealand. Again, during the first World War, prices jumped from 9d. in 1914 to a peak of 1s. 8d. in 1919. After that year prices were so low that many farmers refused to sell, hoping for a rise that never came. Large stocks which deteriorated had, in the end, to be destroyed. Nowadays wool is graded into three or four classes, the best selling at about 17½p a pound.

Other details of expenses are also given. In 1886, 1s. a rood (seven yards) was paid for stone-walling[2]. The same price per rood was paid for "gripping", i.e. surface draining on the moors (done, of course, by hand). Also in the same year they were paying £13 a year wages to the farm-hand, but this did not include board and lodging. The farm-hand got £25 a year in 1891 and £60 in 1928. In 1894, a hay-man received £2.10s. a month; in 1896 £4 and in 1900, £7. In 1940 the hay- man got £12 a month. These casual workers were Irishmen or navvies, who moved about the country in the summer and autumn, hay-making firstly, passing on to the plains for harvesting, and, finally, potato-lifting at the end of the autumn. After the last war Irish farmers used to come over for the hay-harvest, asking up to £60 or £70 a month until a few years ago. Now they are no longer needed as the farms in the dales have become completely mechanized.

In the 1880s and 1890s coals were 8s. a ton, potatoes 5d. a stone, a ham cost 11s. 6d., bacon 7½d a pound and cheese 7½d a pound. Interspersed between items of accounts are odd notes of incidents and landmarks in the life of a dales farmer. During the bad winter of 1895, the farmer "foddered" sheep 166 times and during a snowstorm on 22nd November, 1904, 80 sheep were "over-blown" or buried in the snow. The hardy Swaledale sheep stay on the moors and upper pastures during the winter months except when all the herbage is deep in snow, when they are brought down into the meadows or more sheltered places and fed upon hay.

There is a note in the day-book mentioned earlier that in 1905 the North Riding County Council took over the road from Reeth to Stang Lane top. In the same year piped water was installed in the farmhouse, and a kitchen and bathroom were gradually added later. In 1906 our farmer bought his wife a gramophone for £4.15s. and a 1921 entry states "we got our first car". This was probably one of the first in Swaledale. In 1926 they made their own electricity for lighting purposes and also installed a "swim-bath". This latter was an outside concrete tank which did away with the hand-dipping of sheep. The animals were made to swim through the sheep-dip which filled the tank. This practice was not generally adopted for many years.

[1] Store lambs for fattening.

[2] price today £2 – £3 a yard.

The Swaledale Sheep

FROM THE BEGINNING of the fourteenth century the wealth
and prosperity of Britain depended upon its exports of wool and
woollen cloth to the Continental countries. Until the industrial
revolution of the late eighteenth century, wool, and therefore sheep,
were the main pre-occupation of the men of rural England. Small
mills for spinning and weaving, fulling and dyeing, became established
in the country towns and villages of Yorkshire and in the Eastern and
Western counties. The Cloth-makers' Guilds encouraged expert weavers
from France and Flanders to settle, and gave them special privileges.

Vast flocks were grazed upon the downs and hills, and above
all, along the entire length of the Pennines from Derbyshire to the
Scottish Border. Each area developed its own particular breed.
Leicesters, Lincolns, Southdowns, Suffolks, Cheviots and many others
are known the world over. One particular kind, the "Swaledale",
because of its hardiness and its adaptability to the harsh conditions
of the fells and moorlands, is increasing its popularity amongst the
hill-farmers of the North of England. The origin of the breed is lost
in antiquity.

It is recorded that a transaction took place between AD 1461 and
1471, when the King of Scotland bought (with the consent of the
English King) sheep from Yorkshire for the Royal Forest of Selkirk.
It is extremely likely that the greater part of this flock, if not all,
would be purchased from the two largest sheep-breeders at that
period, the Abbots of Fountains and Rievaulx. Rievaulx Abbey owned
sheep-walks upon their Swaledale estates. Is it possible that this export
of sheep became the original ancestors of the Scottish Blackface breed?

William Marshall, the rural economist, writing in 1794, said that —
    "This Moreland breed of sheep has always been very
different from that of the Vale, and has not varied perhaps
during a succession of the climature, and the extreme coarseness
of the herbage. They live upon the open heaths the year round.
Their food, heath, rushes and a few of the coarsest grasses; a
pasture on which perhaps every other breed of sheep of this

Kingdom would starve."

Horned, black-faced sheep have ranged the Pennines for centuries, particularly around the Yorkshire and Westmorland border. In this isolated area, the local selection of rams and ewes over a long period has led to standardisation, the pure stock of which is now known as the "Swaledale" (named after the Yorkshire Dale in which it was principally reared). In 1919 it was at last recognised as a separate breed, and the "Swaledale Sheep Breeders' Association" was formed to inspect and register the newly-born rams. This Society is now the biggest association of its kind in the country, having the greatest number of annually registered sheep on its books. It began with 159 members, all hill-farmers living within 15 miles of Tan Hill Inn. Tan Hill is the highest "pub" in England. It stands at the junction of three roads — one leading into Westmorland, another into Swaledale and the third into Arkengarthdale. The inn is surrounded by one of the largest expanses of rough grass and heather-clad moorland in the North of England, over which "Swaledales" graze in scattered groups. It is estimated that some two millions of these sturdy, though lightly-built, animals feed upon the northern hills to an altitude of over 2,000 feet.

One important characteristic of the breed is that an individual flock can be trained to become attached or "heughed" (or "heeafed") to that particular piece of moor or fell intended for it. Those animals that do wander are driven back to their companions on the chosen grazing, and in time develop a sense of "belonging" to a certain area, which is never lost. The tendency to stay in a given spot is a psychological trait which has been inherited from the original moorland breed. As most moors and fells are largely unfenced, this habit simplifies the work of the shepherd.

Tenancy contracts between tenant-farmer and landlord, in use since times immemorial, ensure the continuance of this tendency to keep to one area. It is still customary on many farms for the flock to remain an integral part of the landlord's property. The tenant-farmer then pays an annual rent for the sheep, in addition to what he pays for the land and buildings. In return, he gets the use of the flock by selling the surplus progeny and the wool, but he has to leave behind on the moor the original number of sheep at the end of his tenancy.

The "Swaledale" produces an excellent white wool of medium length, which is uniform in character, and although it contains a small amount of grey hair or "kemp" it makes a most durable cloth. In the past it was usually made into rough tweeds and carpets, but now by using the latest technical methods, the fabric is found eminently suitable for the manufacture of high-quality, hard-wearing worsteds and tweeds. The average weight of a ewe's fleece is 3½-4½ lbs. and first-quality wool fetches about 17½p a lb. at the present time. The value of the "Swaledale" as a meat-producing animal has always been recognised. It is an active beast foraging upon a variety of herbs and grasses, so its flesh is sweet and not too fat. The carcase provides medium joints suitable for the small present-day table.

Four-year-old, or draft, ewes, when sold to farmers living on the lower slopes, are usually mated with rams from one of the following "mutton" breeds; Leicesters, Border Leicesters, Teeswaters and Wensleydales. The females of the resultant cross are sought after by farmers of still more fertile land, who again cross them with heavier rams of the "Downs" type, thereby producing lambs almost equivalent in carcase to the "Downs" itself. This method of getting heavy-weight lambs is found more economical than the breeding of heavy pure-bred sheep for flock replacements.

The "wethers", or castrated males, are bought for fattening on the better grazing of the low-lying farms. The ram, or "tup", an attractive animal with large curling horns, is a popular exhibit at all the North Country agricultural shows. A fully grown "tup" has been known to fetch as much as £2,400, while a good "tup" lamb is sold for between £50 and £200.

The Swaledale Sheep-Breeders' Association has now about 900 members residing in all the Yorkshire Dales, Durham, Northumberland, South Westmorland, East Cumberland, Derbyshire and the Cleveland Hills. The breed has also been established as far north as the Isle of Lewis, and cross-bred lambs are being fed on the Norfolk downlands, the Welsh Border and in Devonshire. Enquiries have even been received from the Argentine and India. In 1968, three "tups" were sent to St. Helena to improve the flocks on that island. Whether or not they are successfully "heughed" there, we may hear some day!

Music in the Dale

DALESMEN ARE NOTED for their musical gifts, both vocal and instrumental. In fact a musical tradition has descended in some families from generation to generation. A century or two ago, these talents were expressed by the men who regularly, each Sunday, brought their flutes, fiddles, clarinets, 'cellos, and trombones to church or chapel to accompany the hymn and psalm singing. Each place of worship had its minstrels' gallery or platform for their accommodation.

Minstrels played in Grinton church in 1840. Among them was another Adam Barker of Healaugh. "The Messiah" was performed by Reeth residents, with the help of a few outsiders, at the Wesleyan chapel in 1848. The orchestra consisted of a double bass, violins, flutes and piano.

This coming together of those with musical tastes created a strong fellowship and pride in their contributions to church and chapel services. The situation did not last. During the latter half of the nineteenth century, harmoniums and, later, pipe organs were becoming fashionable, and these were installed in most of the dales churches and chapels. The minstrels' galleries were removed. Alas! the music-makers were no longer required — a sad blow to many village players and to the community life of the dale. After playing for 27 years in Grinton church, Adam Barker gave his bass violin away to a friend. In a latter to the recipient he wrote —

"I was taking the violin into church ... and the parson said, 'Adam! I won't have the fiddle', and I replied, 'You won't have me', and from that day to the present time I have never given anything for church music."

He further wrote —

"The people of Arkendale got a nice new harmonium some years ago and I am told that it is very little used which brings things to my mind in this way — new beesomes sweep clean for a time but are soon thrown aside."

This was in the late 1860s, and it was about this time, and from this musical tradition, that village brass bands were being formed in the dale. The disbanded church and chapel musicians found a new outlet for their talents. By the turn of the century hardly a village or hamlet was without its brass or silver band. Gunnerside may have been the first. Musicians from that place accompanied the copy-holders when they marched over Oxnop Gill Head on their way to vote at the polling booth in Askrigg, at the first Reform Bill election in 1832. At another great event, the opening of the Askrigg railway station in 1877, the Gunnerside band joined the celebrations, arriving in a conveyance drawn by a dozen grey horses.[1] Keld band was also one of the early ones. When the foundation stone of the Thwaite Congregational Chapel was laid in 1863, a procession carrying banners and headed by a brass band left Keld, and, via Angram, marched all the way down to the new site.

Although earlier ones were formed at Keld, Gunnerside, Reeth and Arkengarthdale, (the latter had two at one time!), Muker band has been one of the most successful in the dale. It was formed at a meeting held in 1897 to commemorate Queen Victoria's diamond jubilee. Besson and Company, London, were asked for a price list of second-hand instruments and whether they would exchange two slide trombones for one baritone and one euphonium, any make!   The instruments were eventually bought for £40 and approved by W. Buxton of Gunnerside, who agreed to be the first teacher at two shillings a night for two hours once a week. Each member contributed threepence a night for his tuition. Further instruments were added, and, in June 1897, it was decided to issue a subscription list and collection to cover the initial costs. Heading the list was Captain Lyell (Lord of the Manor), the Reverend J. Cooke (vicar) and James E. Backhouse, with about 200 other subscribers.

The band played at Hardraw in 1900, and the first mentioned appearance at Muker Show was in 1903. One of the annual engage-ments was the Carlton Foresters' March in Coverdale. In 1907 they were carried there and back by Thomas Guy's trap, which cost them thirty shillings. The first leader to be elected was W.T. Raw in 1899, being followed by William Peacock (Bob Bill). In 1946, W. Simm Raw was elected band-master and he carried on until just before he died in 1971. The band competes annually at the Leyburn Festival of Song and often obtains more distinctions than other competing players from as far away as Richmond and Northallerton. It is in great demand at many of the local agricultural shows and at various civic celebrations in the district. W. Simm Raw had the happy knack of recruiting and teaching village boys and youths, thereby ensuring the band's contin-uance.

Many of the older generation of dalesmen will remember Richard Alderson of Keld, commonly known as "Neddy Dick".(2)

He constructed his own pecular percussion instrument, composed of a row of rounded stones collected from the River Swale, each of which, when struck with a hammer, gave its own distinctive note. He was described by a fellow villager:

> "He wer a queer un. He wer brought up to farming: but his mind wer always running on music. He neglected 'isself badly and though he had money he didn't know how to use it. Lots o' fowk came to hear him play on t' stones he had fished up out o' t' beck."

James Reynoldson of Gunnerside left his native village to find work in the cotton mills of Nelson in Lancashire. There he settled with his two brothers. When his son was killed in the first World War, he wrote in his memory two hymn tunes — "Gunnerside" and "Muker". These are often sung in dales Wesleyan Chapels.

The Swaledale Dirge has been collected and harmonised by Fred Burgin from Emanuel White. The first two verses of the Gunnerside version of the dirge came from one of Isaac Watts' hymns published in 1780, but the third and last verse cannot be traced. The origin of the tune is believed to be of great antiquity. Tradition has it that it "dates from the monks".[3]

And finally, changing from the sacred to the profane, is the ballad called "The Swaledale Lad".

[1] "Yorkshire Village", Harley & Ingilby (1953).

[2] He died about 1927.

[3] see "Gunnerside Chapel and Gunnerside Folk" by Margaret Batty, M.A., (pages 29-31).

The Swaledale Lad

When ar was at heam wi' mi dad an'
    mi mam ar niver did have ony fun;
They kept mi garn fra morn till neet,
    si ar thowt fra heam ad run.
Leeds fair a cummin on, ar thowt
    ad hev a spree,
Si ar tacks mi hat and mi **gurt** club
    stick and whistles reet merrilee.
(chorus)   Bumpsy, bumpsy buddy boy,
        Bumpsy, bumpsy boy:
        Bumpsy, bumpsy buddy boy,
        Bumpsy, bumpsy boy.

Ar went into Leeds owd church —
    ar wer niver i' yan i' mi days,
An ar wer maistly ashamed o' misel,
    for ar didn't know their ways;
There wer thirty or forty fowk, i' tubs
    an' boxes sat,
When up cooms a saucy owd fellow,
Says he "Noo, lad tak off thi hat."

(chorus)

Then in ther cooms a great Lord Mayor,
    an' over his shoulders a club,
An' he gat into a white sack poke,
    an got into t' topmost tub,
An' then ther cooms anither chap,
    ar thinks they call'd him Ned,
An he gat into t' bottommost tub,
    an mock'd all t' other chap said,

(chorus)

He wer teachin' rich fowk t' road
    to heaven an t' poor fowk somewhere else,
When up jumps t' chap i' t' bottommost
    tub, says he, "Good fowks, lets sing."
Ar thowt some sang varra weel, while
    others did grunt an' groan,
They all seeam'd to sing what they
    bloomin' well liked,
So I sang "Darby an' Joan".

(chorus)

When preachin' an' prayin' wer ower, an
    fowks wer ganin' away,
Ar went to t' chap i' t' topmost tub —
    says I, "Lad, what's to pay?"
"Why, nowt", says he, "my lad." Begor!
    ar wer right fain!
So ar tacks mi hat an mi gurt club
    stick an' went whislin' oot again.

(chorus)

(A variation of this song was sung in Wensleydale)

Population Figures

Year	Grinton	Reeth	Melbecks	Muker	Marrick	Arkendale	TOTAL
1801	518	1128	1274	1119	474	1186	5699
1811	649	1394	1586	1339	499	1529	6996
1821	689	1460	1726	1425	621	1512	7433
1831	696	1456	1455	1247	659	1446	6959
1841	594	1343	1633	1241	648	1243	6702
1851	598	1344	1661	1321	555	1283	6762
1861	611	1299	1622	1005	462	1147	6146
1871	469	1077	1437	913	412	1018	5326
1881	377	988	1165	837	307	999	4673
1891	280	667	600	615	246	701	3109
1901	262	570	497	549	178	427	2483